Mrs. Earp

Mrs. Earp

The Wives and Lovers of the Earp Brothers

Sherry Monahan

TWODOT®

Guilford, Connecticut
Helena, Montana
An imprint of Globe Pequot Press

A · TWODOT® · BOOK

Copyright © 2013 by Sherry Monahan

Project editor: Lauren Brancato
Layout: Maggie Peterson

Library of Congress Cataloging-in-Publication data is available on file.

ISBN 978-0-7627-8835-4

Printed in the United States of America

10 9 8 7 6 5 4 3 2 1

To the very special women in my family—you make my days brighter with your laughter, support, friendship, and love.
To all of you, especially my mom, Marilyn, my mother-in-law, Veronica, my sister Sue, and my nieces Jamie and Tiffany. I love you all!

Contents

ACKNOWLEDGMENTS

Wow . . . where to begin? So many have helped me in various ways. Roger Jay never hesitated when I asked him for details about the Mrs. Earps. He shared his expertly researched data, his thoughts, and his time. Gary Roberts was also kind and shared his information and thoughts. He also connected me to Roger. To Earp aficionados Jeff Morey and Casey Tefertiller, who have always shared their information with me. To Lyman Hanley, who entrusted me with his Great-Aunt Louisa's letters and photos. To my editors, Erin Turner—thank you for believing in my project—and to Courtney Oppel for her keen eyes and thought-provoking comments!

Special thanks, in alphabetical order, to Nick Cataldo, Anne Collier, Joe Davis (Barton County Historical Society, Lamar, Missouri), Scott Dyke, Marge and Steve Elliott, Chris Enss, Tom Gaumer, Ann Kirschner, Robert McCubbin, Lesa Nichols of the City of San Bernardino/Pioneer Memorial Cemetery, Peoria Public Library, Jim Peterson, Christine Rhodes (*Cochise County Recorder*), Meghan Saar, Alan Smith of the BYU Idaho Family History Center, Fred Sutherland, Marshall Trimble, Kenneth Vail, and Lee Whitney of the Butte–Silver Bow Public Archives.

FOREWORD

I love this country—especially the history and traditions of the West. I come by this love naturally through my family heritage. My grandfather was the actor John Wayne—I am his oldest grandchild. I was very lucky to have spent quite a lot of time with my grandfather. He loved his family very much and shared his time, his love of his country, and his love of Western history with us. We were very blessed. Whenever we could, we spent time on location, at his house, at his ranch, on his boat—and he loved to talk. There was always someone else "special" telling stories, too. Growing up surrounded by real cowboys and their tall tales sends me running to the bookstore or movie theater when a new Western story comes out.

My love of the West led me to be involved in the Western Heritage Awards at the National Cowboy and Western Heritage Museum in Oklahoma City. Their annual awards honor outstanding writers, filmmakers, artists, poets, singers, and actors who preserve the values and traditions of the Western way of life. My reason for this explanation is that it was the scene of my first meeting with the author of this book, Sherry Monahan. While presenting her with a Wrangler Award for her appearance in a History Channel program called *Cowboys and Outlaws: Wyatt Earp*, we became fast friends over our love of history—especially the wild, Wild West—the fabulous stories of the people who settled this country we both love, and our love of the Earp brothers.

While Sherry was on the West Coast doing research for her book *California Vines, Wines & Pioneers*, she told me about her book on the Earp women. She mentioned a story about my grandfather and Wyatt Earp. During her research, Sherry said, she'd heard Wyatt had been on the set of a few John Ford movies, and my grandfather had modeled one of his characters on Wyatt Earp. Even though his meeting with Earp was very brief, he was an avid reader of historical fiction and nonfiction and listened closely to the stories of all of those wranglers and stuntmen on the sets. The actors who were very close to Earp were Tom Mix and William S. Hart, who were a bit older than my granddad. Probably most of his direction and knowledge came from John Ford, who also met Earp. I can tell you his library was filled with books on all the well-known lawmen and outlaws of the West. John Wayne would have admired any person who would put his own life in harm's way to protect the lives and rights of others—especially those of his family.

Sherry's book became even more intriguing to me because of the personal connection. Wyatt Earp was not only a good friend to both Tom Mix and William S. Hart, he was a regular fixture and adviser on many of the early Western movie sets. During the summer and on the weekends while we were growing up, the studio back lots or location sets were our playgrounds. We pretended to have shootouts at the OK Corral, making our way across the canyons and mountains, and back and forth to Tombstone. What an exciting concept that now we'll know more about the Earp women.

There are not many books about the women of the West, and certainly none that include all the Earp women under one cover. In *Mrs. Earp: The Wives and Lovers of the Earp Brothers,* the reader will finally learn about the women who followed these famous lawmen into the untamed frontier towns and sometimes had to leave them in pine boxes. Sherry's diligent genealogical research provides information on the women who have been in the shadows and sheds light on some who were previously unknown. The lives these women chose were hard; some of them were prostitutes, and it appears some of the brothers allowed their wives to continue working in this capacity. Just like their husbands' lives, some of the stories about the women were mysterious, and some remain that way. The popular movies about Wyatt Earp have told us a little about the women in the lives of Wyatt and Virgil, including Aurilla, Mattie, Josie, and Allie, but very little about the rest of the brothers' spouses except for their devotion to the Earp brothers and their migration west. The women of the Earp family helped to shape the famous brothers' lives. Hopefully the rest of them will become as well-known as the brothers they married.

—Anita La Cava Swift

INTRODUCTION

When most people hear the name Earp, they think of Wyatt, Virgil, Morgan, and sometimes the lesser known James and Warren—in that order, which is how you'll see them in this book. They also had a half-brother named Newton, who lived a fairly quiet, uneventful life. While it's true these men made history on their own, they all had a Mrs. Earp behind them—some more than one.

For those who aren't familiar with the Earp brothers, let me introduce you to them and share some highlights, along with some details about the most pivotal time in their lives in Tombstone, Arizona. These men came from a close-knit family and were there to back each other up—no matter the situation. Their lives were intertwined from their childhood to the boomtown days. More often than not, you could find at least two, if not more, of the Earp brothers living in the same town, despite the fact that they moved around like gypsies.

According to Mrs. Virgil Earp, when news reached Virgil in Prescott, Arizona, that a big silver strike was found in Tombstone, he sent letters to his brothers to join him. It would be that news that would forever alter the lives of the Earp brothers and their wives in ways they could never imagine. They arrived in Tombstone in late 1879 just as the boom was beginning and settled in. They began buying mining claims and because of their law enforcement backgrounds, they had a few opportunities in Tombstone. Wyatt became Pima County's Deputy Sheriff in July 1880 for Charles Shibell, and Virgil, who was already a US deputy marshal, became the acting town marshal when Fred White was killed by Curly Bill Brocious that same year.

Tombstone not only had regular town folk and businesses, but also had a lawless element that frequently visited and harassed the locals. Curly Bill Brocious, John Ringo, the Clantons, and the McLaurys were known as the "cowboy" element in town. They were known cattle rustlers and, when drunk, tended to get loud in town. An 1887 *Police Gazette* article described just how ruthless they were:

> *. . . a whole band of out-lawed cutthroats who had sought a safe refuge in Arizona's mountainous ranges. . . . They had until the advent of Earp and his three brothers done as they pleased, murdering and robbing with none to molest. This organization of the famous bandits was headed by the notorious "Curly Bill." They had for several years kept the portion of Arizona in which Tombstone is situated completely terrorized. The law was defied and the officials powerless to enforce it. Citizens were made to throw up their hands in broad daylight and hand over whatever of value they possessed. Wells, Fargo & Co. were at the mercy of these highway men, and many times their coaches were "held up" and their treasury box handed down to the merciless villains who did not hesitate to kill, when their demands were not complied with.*
>
> *The express company officials had heard the Earp boys spoken of as a set of very resolute men, who had been officers of the law. They determined upon securing the services of at least one of them to act in the capacity of "shotgun" messenger. The duty of the messenger would be to protect the treasury box while in transit to the railroad at Benson, some thirty miles distant. Morgan Earp was accordingly employed, and it is needless to add that after he had assumed charge of the treasury box robberies became less frequent. Morgan's acceptance of position in the express company's employ was, however, the signal for an open declaration of war between the robbers and Earp boys. The cowboys declared that unless "Morg" Earp gave up his job as messenger they would "kill him." This declaration they made known to "Morg." The latter sent them word that he intended pursuing the even tenor of his way, and that any time they saw fit to kill him all they had to do was to commence hostilities. This so enraged the*

outlaw element that they concluded one day to beard the lion in his den and see what kind of mettle the Earps were made of.[1]

By September 1880 the Earps had already become the enemy of the cowboys when a well-liked dandy arrived in Tombstone named John "Johnny" Behan. Behan had been in other parts of the territory and was politically connected. So when he learned a new county was being formed and Tombstone would be its seat, he saw opportunities and lit out for the silver mining town.

During the Pima County Sheriff elections massive fraud was found in the run between Charles Shibell and Bob Paul. Wyatt Earp resigned to support Bob Paul, and he and his brothers were successfully making money at their mining ventures. When it was announced that Cochise County was looking for a new sheriff, both Wyatt and Johnny Behan wanted the position. Behan approached Wyatt and said if he didn't run and Behan won, he would appoint Wyatt as his undersheriff. The Cochise County sheriff position was a lucrative proposition and received a portion of the taxes collected in the county. Wyatt never ran for the position and when Behan won, he chose Harry Woods instead of Wyatt. With bad blood between the Earps and the cowboys and now between Wyatt and Johnny Behan, who supported the cowboys, it was just a matter of time before tempers, pride, and indignation got the best of all involved. By October 1881 the cowboys were publicly threatening the Earps, and the Earps were ready to defend themselves and uphold the law.

With the town hearing rumors that the cowboys were ready to have a go at the Earps, Virgil, acting as city marshal, along with his brothers Wyatt and Morgan who received special appointments as policemen, and their friend John Henry "Doc" Holliday, had no choice but to go out and meet the cowboys face to face. The Earps and Holliday proceeded to the empty lot behind the OK Corral to disarm the cowboys who were illegally carrying weapons in town. Some thirty bullets flew in less than twenty-five seconds, and the town quickly became divided about who was right and who was wrong. Tombstone chronicler Clara Brown described the incident:

The inmates of every house in town were greatly startled by the sudden report of firearms, about 3 p.m., discharged with such lightning-like rapidity that it could be compared only to the explosion of a bunch of firecrackers; and the aspect of affairs grew more portentous when, a few moments later, the whistles of the steam hoisting works sounded a shrill alarm. "The cowboys!" cried some, thinking that a party of those desperadoes were "taking the town." "The Indians," cried a few of the most excitable. Then, after it was learned that a fight had been engaged in between Marshal Earp, his two brothers, a special deputy (Doc Holliday), and four cowboys . . . speculation as to the cause of the affray ran riot. In the midst of this, when the scene upon the streets was one of intense excitement, the whistle again sounded, and directly well-armed citizens appeared from all quarters, prepared for any emergency. This revealed, what was not before generally known, the existence of a "Vigilance Committee," composed of law abiding citizens, who organized with the determination of upholding right and combating wrong, and who agreed upon a signal of action from the mines. Their services were not needed, however, on this occasion.[2]

When the smoke cleared, Frank and Tom McLaury were dead; Billy Clanton died shortly thereafter. Although Wyatt escaped unharmed, his brothers Virgil and Morgan Earp were wounded. Wyatt and his friend Doc Holliday were arrested, and a lengthy preliminary hearing ensued.

According to Judge Spicer, who presided over the hearing, Virgil Earp, as Chief of Police, Morgan and Wyatt Earp, and Doc Holliday, whom Virgil called upon for help, went to the site of the fight, near the OK Corral, for the purpose of arresting and disarming the Clantons and McLaurys. He did not feel there was enough evidence to support a trial. The "cowboys" did not feel justice had been served and they took matters into their own hands. In December, they made an unsuccessful assassination attempt on Virgil Earp that crippled him for life, and in March 1882, they murdered Morgan Earp.

After the murder of his younger brother Morgan, Wyatt went on a revenge ride that the newspapers coined "The Vendetta." Fearing justice would not be served and spurred on by the pain of losing a close sibling, Wyatt went on a killing spree. His posse, which included his youngest brother Warren, hunted down three of the men implicated in the shootings and then they left the territory pursued by a posse led by Johnny Behan.

Although there seem to be as many variations of the Earps' Tombstone chapter as there are storytellers, all accounts tend to have one thing in common: the noticeable absence of the women in the Earp's lives. The Earp men, starting with the patriarch of the Earp clan, Nicholas Porter Earp, did not like being alone. Nicholas Earp was married three times, with his last marriage being at the age of eighty, his bride being fifty-three. Three of his sons would follow their father's lead and marry more than once. It's also possible these Earp brothers had additional brides or lovers that have yet to be discovered!

This book collectively introduces you to the lives of the known women who shared the title of Mrs. Earp either by name or relationship. Some of these women may have helped shape the future of the Earp brothers and may have even been the fuel behind some of the fires they encountered.

It's interesting to note that while these brothers collectively had eleven wives, only Virgil, and possibly Wyatt, ever fathered a child. James's wife Bessie is the only Mrs. Earp to have had children, but they were with her first husband when she was young. Were the Mrs. Earps sterile, were they all just that unlucky, did they practice abstinence, or was it something else? It's also possible some had miscarriages, or "abortions," which was the common term in the 19th century. Several dictionaries of the day, including Webster's, defined abortion as "an act of miscarrying."

Another reason for their lack of children could have been from their own doing. Not all Victorian women, especially working girls, wanted to be pregnant. There were a few options for them, which included drinking herbal concoctions or nasty medicines. The other was physical and much more gruesome. There were no clinics, and while not illegal until the late 1800s in most states, abortions were not looked upon favorably. Women had to find midwives or doctors who were willing. More often than not, the pregnancy went away, but sometimes the mother did as well. If she did survive, she may have lost the ability to have any more children because of the procedure.

In the 1904 book *Dr. Chase's Last Recipe Book and Household Physician* it states, "Sometimes for wicked purposes, it is attempted to procure abortion, either by strong and acrid medicines, by violent exercises, or by direct application to the parts concerned . . . and that to procure abortion . . . is to run the risk of a speedy death. . . ."

According to Earp researcher Scott Dyke, Josephine Earp told her biographer Mabel Cason that she had two or maybe three "abortions" after she left Tombstone. Since the word "abortion" was used differently than we use it today, was Josephine stating she miscarried two or three times or did she mean the other? We can never truly know.

Documentation has been discovered for only three of the women who called themselves Mrs. Earp, which proved they were legally married. Oddly enough, these three women are historical mysteries. The other women called themselves Mrs. Earp, but may or may not have been legally married. It was very easy in Victorian times to simply become man and wife—not many questioned a relationship. Despite a piece of paper—or lack thereof—these Earp women were considered wives during that era. Unlike modern times, frontier marriages were often quick, informal affairs with the bride simply wearing her best dress. A justice of the peace presided over the quick ceremony, and the witnesses may or may not have been friends or family.

Whether they worked as soiled doves or stayed at home, with one exception or two, the Earp women acted no differently from other housewives of their day. They cooked meals, washed and ironed clothes, made beds, swept floors, played games, wrote letters, and took care of their husbands. They didn't involve themselves in politics or their husbands' business affairs. For the most part, they followed their husbands from town to town and did what they were told. It's easy to imagine all of the Mrs. Earps as glorified madams or gunslinging sidekicks to their husbands. It's true a couple did fit that profile, but most were just ordinary women looking for love and stability. They lived hard lives as frontier women and at least four of them died before the age of fifty.

The Earp name has stirred up many a historical controversy over the years, from false photos to false accounts and so much more. With any history, there is bound to be controversy simply because it can be a jigsaw puzzle. The Earp field is especially difficult because so much of the historical information is in private collections. Some of these collections include rare photos, letters, journals, and more, but are often difficult to access or come with strings attached. In addition, some of this data has been interpreted by its current owner and then shared through that perspective. For any researcher, seeing the raw documentation is a must. As you investigate and dig up as many firsthand accounts as you can, you piece them all together to get the most complete picture. From there, you try to tell the correct story—but even using old firsthand accounts can be misleading. I've used my skills as a professional genealogist to piece together the lives of these women with the hopes of looking at them from a different perspective.

I, like many others, have heard the names of some of the Earp women and seen them portrayed in movies, but knew very little about them. Working on this book introduced me to them. Virgil's wife Allie made me laugh out loud; Morgan's wife Louisa made me appreciate life; Wyatt's fourth wife, Josephine, proved to be the most difficult, but only because she did a great deal of yarn-spinning to cover up her past. I pitied her and supported her at the same time. For her, I just tried to take the information she provided and prove which portions of her story were the most plausible. Josephine, like so many people from the past, may have felt shame about her chosen path, but I don't feel we have any right to judge the decisions of those who lived over a hundred years ago. We truly cannot understand or fully know what circumstances caused them to make the choices they did. Let us not judge them, but rather consider their situations and get to know them, for better or worse.

Having said all that, I've done my own genealogical research on these women, but also used books, some old and some new, to help me in writing this book. This is not meant to be a scholarly work, but an easy-to-read nonfiction book that focuses the spotlight on the Earp women. Until now they have been mentioned in books about their husbands, and a couple had their stories told, but no one has put all of them in one book together. I felt it was time they received some much-needed attention. This book may not have many new details about the Mrs. Earps, but at least they're being given their due. Sadly, because of the times in which they lived, some of the Earp wives left behind only mere mentions of their lives. Details about who they were and what happened to them remain a mystery, despite extensive research. I chose to include the wives of the Earp men who lived in Tombstone, Arizona, at one time or another. I decided it was high time to bring them out from behind the shadows of the men who have captured our imaginations for so long. Surely the women closest to those men had their own interesting stories to tell. I only hope I have done justice to Aurilla, Sarah, Celia Ann, Josephine, Magdalena, Rozilla, Alvira, Louisa, Bessie, and Kate—all better known as Mrs. Earp.

CHAPTER ONE

Mr. & Mrs. Wyatt Earp

"From the moment that my restless young feet first touched the hospitable Embarcadero at San Francisco, life has been a fascinating and often exciting adventure."
—JOSEPHINE SARAH MARCUS-EARP

Wyatt Earp was a man of many occupations and a few wives and the best known of the Earp brothers. He's the brother most written about in history books and featured in movies and on TV. He was born March 19, 1848, in Monmouth, Illinois, to native North Carolinian Nicholas Porter Earp and Victoria "Virginia" Ann Cooksey-Earp. Wyatt was the third son of the couple, who were married on July 30, 1840, in Ohio County, Kentucky. His father was restless, a trait he would pass down to his sons, and moved his family often. In 1850 Wyatt's parents moved to Lake Prairie, Iowa, where Nicholas worked as a cooper and farmer. Ten years later the Earps were residing in Pella, Iowa, where Wyatt attended school. Sometime in 1869 Wyatt and his family moved to Lamar, Missouri, and in November 1869, Nicholas became justice of the peace and Wyatt was appointed to his father's old position as constable. Then when Lamar was incorporated in the spring of 1870, Wyatt became Lamar City constable after a special election to choose officials until the regular election could be held in November. His half-brother, Newton, ran against him.

In Lamar, Wyatt met the woman who would become his first wife: Aurilla Sutherland. When people familiar with Wyatt Earp think of his wife, they tend to recall his last wife, Josephine, but long before Wyatt met Josephine in Tombstone, Aurilla Sutherland became the first Mrs. Wyatt Earp. The woman, and her name, is a mystery. Her name has been commonly thought to be Urilla, but there is no proof of any variation. The 1850 census lists it as Aurilla, while the 1860 census lists her first name as Arilla and her last name as Southerland. The 1870 census lists her as Rilla, which is a nickname for Aurilla or Aurelia.

Aurilla was the second daughter and sixth child of William Sutherland, dubbed "Uncle Billy" by the Lamar locals, and Permelia Farris-Sutherland, who were both originally from New York. She was born on January 10, 1850, in Ela, Lake County, Illinois, and lived there until she was at least ten years old. By the time she was twenty she and her family were residing in Lamar, Missouri, where the population was about 1,600, including Wyatt Earp and his family.

Founded in 1852, Lamar saw all but seven of its buildings destroyed during the Civil War. But by the late 1860s, when the Earp family arrived in town, a construction boom was in full swing. Businesses were going up and a temporary courthouse was established on the west side of the town square, along with a bank. Several other buildings dotted the north side.

There's no proof how the couple met, but Aurilla could have met Wyatt in a few ways. In a town that small and with Wyatt being the constable, she may have met him in town, where her father owned William's Exchange Hotel on the town square near the courthouse. Wyatt's father also owned a bakery and sold oysters just three doors down from the Sutherlands' hotel. The Sutherland family and the Earps did not live far from one another either, so a neighborhood connection is also possible. Since both families were Methodist, they could have met in church, where a close-knit town like Lamar was bound to have Sunday gatherings after services. Lamar's Methodist Episcopal church was founded in 1865 but didn't have a building until

Wyatt Earp posed for this photo circa 1880 in Tombstone, Arizona, where he lived until the murder of his brother Morgan in 1882.

COURTESY OF ROBERT G. MCCUBBIN

about 1870. Around this time, several of Lamar's churches, including the Methodist Episcopal, did not have buildings yet, so they held services in the courthouse on the west side of the square. Regardless of how Aurilla met Wyatt, the couple were married on January 16, 1870, in her father's hotel. The *Southwest Missourian* wrote of William and his hotel, "Uncle Billy, lively and full of fun—singing or whistling that same old tune."[3]

On August 28 Wyatt bought a quaint little house valued at $75 two doors down from his parents and next door to his half-brother Newton's, and worked as the town's constable. It was in this house that he and Aurilla began their life together. Seemingly, Aurilla and Wyatt settled into a typical Victorian life. While her husband worked, Aurilla cooked, cleaned, and kept the house like all other ladies of her time did.

According to the September 3, 1870, census, Wyatt and his wife were alive and well. All that changed when Aurilla suddenly died around October or November of that same year. While it's generally known she died, no death records exist, nor do any that indicate how or exactly when she died, but given the timing of their marriage and her death, it's possible she died in childbirth. There have been other rumors that she died during a typhus epidemic. According to Joe Davis of the Barton County Historical Society in Lamar, Missouri, "As far as the typhoid in the 1870s, yes. It was a problem around here all the way up until the early twentieth century. Not a huge problem or epidemic, but several people had died from it."

It is strange the local paper never carried any details of her death, especially since her father's hotel was extremely close to the paper's office. The town was not that big and surely they knew Uncle Billy Sutherland and his daughter, as well as Wyatt Earp and his justice of the peace father. So what happened to Aurilla that neither the local paper nor her family wanted anyone to know? It could be that the

Lamar newspaper printed only what wasn't widely known and didn't feel the need to print items everyone in town knew about, such as Aurilla's death.

Stories of a street fight between the Earp brothers and possibly the Brummett brothers, which took place after her death, could lead to other speculations. Maybe something was amiss and her brothers grew angry over it. It's quite possible there was tension between the families that began in 1869. In April that year, William Sutherland was arrested, but the indictment was quashed. He was later arrested on three counts of selling liquor. Additional unknown charges were filed against Norman Young, John Cones, and William Sutherland on April 15, 1870.[4] Nicholas would have been justice of the peace, with Wyatt as constable at this time. On top of all that, Nicholas was paid $4.00 and Wyatt was paid $9.30 in a case against "Granville Brummett and others" on August 5, 1870.[5]

If in fact the street fight took place, it must have occurred shortly after Aurilla's funeral, because her brother Frederick was living in Osage Mission (now St. Paul), Kansas, in July 1870. Since Fred was involved in the fight, he must have been home to attend his sister's funeral.

Aurilla's brother Fred was known for his temper. During a personal interview, his grandson Fred Sutherland told me, "To understand my picture of Grandpa Fred, you must understand my picture of my dad, Jim—just as understanding any story depends upon your credible knowledge of the storyteller. Jim was complex; aren't we all? He was a knight errant, searching for glory, fame, or riches, in that order. I believe he inherited this quest from Grandpa Fred. He could be incredibly charming to women, but he treated them disrespectfully. I also sense that this was learned or inherited from his dad. Competition was everything to him. Again, like father, like son, I believe."

Since we know so little about Aurilla, knowing something of her brother might shed some light on her family life. Regarding

Frederick Sutherland was the brother of Aurilla Sutherland, Wyatt's first wife.

his grandfather's competitive nature, Fred's grandson also shared, "Grandpa Fred was a great sprinter and was the first US marshal of Pittsburg, Kansas. And that was before Wyatt Earp was marshal in Dodge City. This one is one of the most curious events I have ever experienced. My dad mentioned some town in Kansas (it may have been Frontenac) that had really good baseball players who always won their games. Next he tells me that his dad, Fred, and his team went there to play against them. While everyone expected Frontenac to win, my grandpa's team came out on top. Then my dad says that Grandpa and his team walked down the main street of this town and sang a victory song . . . and my dad sang it, word for word to me! My math would indicate that this game should have taken place in around 1870 when Grandpa would have been about twenty years old. The words were something like, 'We are the boys from Columbus! We beat the boys from (unknown). No one thought we could do it. Aren't we great?' It was two or three stanzas of music, but that is the gist of it. I still don't know what to make of it."

If in fact Jim was like his father, Fred, then could it not also be true that Aurilla's brother Fred was like his father, William? If so, then Aurilla was born into a male-dominant, competitive family life, and her father likely treated her with little respect.

According to the Barton County Historical Society's Joe Davis, Aurilla is buried in the southeast corner of Howell Cemetery, Barton County, Missouri. Joe said, "All of the Sutherlands had very nice headstones in Lake Cemetery west of town, so why didn't Aurilla? Even the Sutherlands' baby who died at a very early age had a stone. It really makes no sense that she was buried way out of town in Howell Cemetery."

It's interesting to note that on November 8, 1870, Wyatt was appointed constable, and the day *before* he had sold his house and listed himself as single. This sudden sale seems timely with Aurilla's estimated death date. Once Aurilla was gone, Wyatt left his Victorian, white-picket-fence life and Lamar for good.

Aurilla's sudden death, coupled with a possible fraud scandal while Wyatt acted as constable, are possibly what caused him to leave Lamar and take up a seedier lifestyle. Likely suffering from the pain and shock of his wife's death, Wyatt began breaking the law rather than enforcing it. Facing embezzlement charges, Wyatt fled Lamar in late 1870 and made his way to Indian Territory, now eastern Oklahoma.

Aurilla Sutherland's grave in Howell Cemetery in Lamar, Missouri
COURTESY OF SCOTT DYKE

In 1871 Wyatt and companions Edward Kennedy and John Shown were charged with larceny for stealing two horses valued at $100 each from William and James Keys on March 28. Shown's wife, Anna, gave a deposition stating Earp and Kennedy got her husband drunk and convinced him to help them. She also went along for the ride, and recounted, "They got my husband drunk near Ft. Gibson about the 28th of March 1871. . . . They told him to ride 50 miles towards Kansas and then they would meet him and then they would put up the horses to another wagon and he could ride. I went with these two men and met my husband 50 miles north of Ft. Gibson. . . . Earp drove on for three nights (we laid over days) about 3 o'clock of the third night, James M. Keys overtook us. My husband said he could have the horses—the other defendants Earp and Kennedy told Keys that my husband stole the horses." In April they were arrested and ordered to "find bail" in the amount of $500. While Kennedy stood trial and was acquitted, Shown and Earp escaped from the Van Buren, Arkansas, jail on May 8, 1871, with five other men. Deputy US marshals pursued them, but Earp and Shown were never caught. Between 1851 and 1871, the seat of the Federal Court for the Western District of Arkansas was located at Van Buren. In March 1871 Congress passed an act moving the federal court seat, but it was three more months until court opened in Fort Smith.

By 1872 Wyatt had made his way to Peoria, Illinois, where he apparently continued his downward spiral into the depths of depravity. He appears in *Root's Peoria City Directory, 1872* and is listed as living at the same residence as a notorious madam named Jane Haspel (aka Haspill or Hackell) on Washington Street. He and Jane were both listed as working on Hamilton Street, which is where police arrested both of them at "Haspel's brothel on Hamilton." Wyatt wasn't the first Earp brother to have contact with Jane in Peoria, and while Wyatt was still in Lamar, his brother Virgil had moved to Peoria, where Jane had a place on Maple Street. Wyatt continued his less-than-respectable life in Peoria and appears to have been in charge of, or possibly a partner in, Jane's brothel. On February 24, 1872, Wyatt and his brother Morgan were arrested for "Keeping and Being Found in a House of Ill-Fame," according to the local newspaper. Author Steve Gatto noted, "Four women and three men were arrested in the bagnio bust. It was the latest effort of Mayor Peter Brotherson's police, led by Chief Samuel L. Gill, to quash prostitution." The *Peoria Daily Transcript* reported on February 27, 1872, "George Randall, Wyatt Earp, and Morgan Earp, three men arrested at the Haspell bagnio on Hamilton street, Saturday evening last, were brought before Justice Cunningham, yesterday to answer to the charge of being found in a house of ill fame . . . the men were fined $20.00 each and costs." A few months later, on May 9, Wyatt and Morgan were arrested again, but at a different brothel. On May 11, 1872, Peoria's *Daily Transcript* reported, "That hotbed of iniquity, the McClellan Institute on Main Street, near Water, was pulled on Thursday night, and quite a number of inmates transient and otherwise were found therein. Wyat [*sic*] Earp and his brother Morgan Earp, were each fined $44.55 and as they had not the money and would not work, they languished in the cold and silent calaboose." Four months later the *Peoria Daily National Democrat* reported another arrest of Wyatt at a brothel.

It appears Wyatt met his next wife while in Peoria. It's quite possible a sixteen-year-old Illinois girl named Sarah Haspel, daughter of Madam Jane Haspel, was the second wife of Wyatt Earp. By all appearances, Sarah Haspel's relationship with Wyatt was the polar opposite of Aurilla's. Rather than a marriage record showing their union, Sarah is linked to Wyatt by an arrest. In fact, the arrest of Sarah and Wyatt was reported in the September 10, 1872, edition of the *Peoria Daily National Democrat:* "Some of the women are reported to be good looking, but all appear to be terribly depraved. John Walton, the skipper of the boat, and Wyatt Earp, the Peoria bummer, were each fined $43.15. . . . Sarah Earp, alias Sally Heckell, calls herself the wife of Wyatt." So, was she really his wife, or just a prostitute using her boss's last name? Since she traveled with Wyatt after they left Peoria, she appears to have been his wife. Her alias of Sally was not uncommon, since Sally and Sadie are nicknames for the given name of Sarah, and it wasn't uncommon for soiled doves of the day to change their first names.

The 1870 US census did not turn up any results for Sally Heckell, but it did record a Sally Haskel living in a house of ill repute and working as a prostitute. That same census also indicated that a ten-year-old girl named Mary Haspel worked in that same house as a domestic. In a highly unusual move, the census taker wrote next to her name, "May God pity you." Jane Haspel was a Peoria madam with whom both Wyatt and Virgil were known to associate, and who had daughters named Sarah and Mary. While Jane was not listed as living with her daughters, she was in Peoria at the time and she appeared in the *Peoria City Directory*. Sarah also had a brother named Edward who may have been with Jane when the census was taken. Again, census takers often wrote names how they heard them, and Haskel and Haspel sound alike.

Nothing on paper appears to indicate a troubled childhood for Jane, so what motivated her to force her daughter or possibly daughters into prostitution? Jane was born in eastern Tennessee around 1832, and her father, Noah Hammick, was a woodchopper. Her mother, Elizabeth, performed typical housewife duties and cared for the family while Noah worked. In 1850 eighteen-year-old Jane—along with her nine-year-old brother, Peter, and their baby sister, Martha, who was just ten months old—was living at home. Their family situation appears to have been quite typical, but then again, names, dates, and places on paper are merely a generic snapshot of anyone's invariably complex history.

Jane married Sarah's father, German immigrant Frederick Haspel, who was born in Württemberg, Germany, on April 23, 1824. He was a blue-eyed, sandy-haired Catholic boy who stood five-foot-seven. Although no records indicate when he and/or his family arrived in America, it is known that Frederick was a butcher by trade and enlisted in the army on March 6, 1851. However, in May that same year, he was listed as having deserted at Fort Leavenworth. There's a discrepancy as to when Frederick married Jane. The marriage was recorded on October 30, 1852, in McLean County, Illinois, but a judge later stated it was September 15, 1854. Sarah was their first child, but it's hard to determine her exact date of birth because of the discrepancy regarding her parents' marriage date. However, according to the age listed on her death certificate, Sarah was born in 1853, which means the October 30, 1852, marriage date is correct or Sarah was born out of wedlock. Her brother, Edward, was born around 1858 and her sister, Mary, around 1860.

When the Civil War broke out, Frederick joined the Union army in Bloomington on October 11, 1861, as a private in Company B, 39th Illinois Infantry Regiment. On December 22, 1863, he was discharged because of an injury that would later cause him to lose his left leg above the knee. He never returned to Jane and his family.

Illiterate and left alone to care for three children, Jane turned to the only thing she could find that would pay enough to provide for her family: prostitution. In 1865, Emma Jane Haspel listed herself in a Peoria City directory as the widow of Frederick and was living on Harrison Street. Despite listing herself as a widow, she was not. By 1870, Jane had dropped her first given name, no longer declared herself a widow, and simply went by Mrs. Jane Haspel.

Frederick refused to acknowledge his wife or children and claimed Jane had deserted him. When he was admitted to the Northwestern Branch of the National Home for Disabled Volunteer Soldiers in Milwaukee, Wisconsin, in 1867, he listed himself as a single man.

He visited the home off and on until 1892 and worked as a butcher in Madison, Wisconsin. He began a new family when he married a woman named Carolina in 1884.

When Jane filed for divorce from Frederick on May 13, 1871, she claimed he had deserted her on March 1, 1864. In an amended complaint, filed June 15, 1872, by her attorneys, Jane claimed that Frederick had been guilty of "repeated cruelty" toward her, and "on the 1st day of January 1865 the said Frederick Haspel struck beat choked & kicked the complainant and neglected to furnish her with the necessary food and clothing for herself & children, and again on the 1st day of May 1865 the said Frederick Haspel struck, kicked, choked, & beat your complainant, striking her a severe blow in the face, knocking her down & [*illegible*] injuring her."

For reasons unknown, the divorce judge stated the Haspels were lawfully married on September 15, 1854, and decreed that "they had as the issue of said marriage three children to wit: Sarah now aged 17 years, Edward now aged 15 years & Mary now aged 13 years." The judge—possibly named S. S. Ruhmund, although the spelling is questionable—then found Frederick to be an unfit father and awarded the divorce and custody of the children to Jane. There's no date on the judge's decree, but it came in the May term of the circuit court.

Jane's daughter Sarah remained in the only profession she knew and by early 1874 she and Wyatt rolled into the rip-roaring cattle town of Wichita, Kansas, along with Wyatt's older brother James and his wife, Bessie. In a letter to his biographer Stuart Lake, Wyatt stated, "Mr. Caines said I came to Wichita in seventy-three, but it(s) a mistake in his fact. I arrived in Wichita direct from my Buffalo hunt in seventy-four. Mr. Caines also was wrong about my being hired in the police force by Mike Meagher. Bill Smith was the Marshal who hired me in. And Mike Meagher was elected Marshal the following spring."

Municipal records listed a prostitute named Sally Earp who operated a brothel with Wyatt's sister-in-law Bessie from January 1874 to April 1876. In early May 1874 Sarah (Sallie per the records) was fined $8 for being a prostitute, along with James Earp's wife, Bessie. On June 3, 1874, Sarah and Bessie were arrested on a complaint from Samuel A. Martin that they "set up and keep a bawdy house or brothel and did appear and act as Mistresses and have the case and management of a certain one story frame building situated and located north of Douglas Avenue near the bridge leading across the Arkansas River used and kept by said parties as a house of prostitution in the city of Wichita, Sedgwick County and aforesaid contrary to the Statutes of Kansas made and provided." The ladies were arrested the same day and pleaded guilty to the charge. Since they did not have the $250 for bail money, they were locked up. They eventually got the money and were released. On September 15, 1874, their attorney, William Baldwin, had the case dismissed. Between then and February 1875, Sally was fined several more times for prostitution. Wyatt seems to have walked a fine line between upholding the law and breaking it. According to the *Wichita Eagle*, Wyatt was appointed as a police officer in Wichita, Kansas, in April 1875 under Deputy City Marshal John Behrens. After Wyatt joined the law force Sarah never appeared in the police or court records again—or anywhere else, for that matter. When the Kansas state census was taken in April 1875, Wyatt, James, and Bessie were all there, but Sarah was not. It's possible this is around the time she disappeared from Wyatt's life.

Historical records do provide small details about what happened to Edward and Jane Haspel. After her divorce was granted, Jane married Charles Clisby in 1872, but he was arrested on unknown charges shortly thereafter and was sent to prison. While neither Sarah nor her mother, Jane, is found in any records for 1879, Sarah's brother, Edward, is. He's listed in *Root's Peoria City Directory* for 1879 and 1880 as a teamster. Then, in the 1880 US census, Edward and Jane were recorded as residing in Kansas City, Missouri. He was also listed in a Peoria city directory in 1881 working as a laborer and living on Water Street. In 1882, a Kansas City business directory listed Jane Haspel as the widow of Frederick, living with her son Edward at 1509 E. 18th Street, but there is no mention of Sarah or her sister, Mary. It's curious that Jane went back to declaring Frederick as her departed husband.

The following year Sarah appeared in the Kansas City directory under the name of Sadie Haspel, living on Main Street, but neither her mother nor her brother were listed. Edward additionally shows up in Kansas City, Missouri, business directories for 1885, 1887, and 1891, when he worked as a dog catcher.

According to research by noted Earp enthusiast Roger Jay, details uncovered in pension records indicate that Sarah visited her father in Milwaukee several times during the 1880s and 1890s. During a visit in 1891 Sarah mentioned that her mother had died sometime before 1891. And per Frederick's pension records, her stepmother stated that Sarah lived with a prizefighter named Murphy during that time. However, she ended up marrying a man named Bollman. When Sadie Bollman died on July 29, 1919, she was a widow who had been living in the Chicago suburb of Oak Forest. It's very likely Sadie Bollman was Sarah Haspel, because the death record indicates she was born in 1853 in Illinois and her mother was Jane Haspel. Both of those details match Sarah Haspel Earp's. She's buried in the Catholic Mt. Olivet Cemetery in Chicago, but she has no headstone and is buried alone. It's interesting to note that Sarah did not keep the Earp name after she and Wyatt parted ways, and she started calling herself Sadie.

Either Sarah left Wyatt or he left her, but there is no proof of either. Around May 1876 Wyatt made his way to the cow town of Dodge City, Kansas. It appears that Wyatt was a phoenix in Dodge

City, where he rose from the hellish ashes in which he had buried himself where he resided in Dodge as an upstanding lawman until March 1877. He disappeared for a few months but returned on July 7, 1877, when the *Dodge City Times* reported, "Wyatt Earp, who was on our city police force last summer, is in town again. We hope he will accept a position on the force once more. He had a quiet way of taking the most desperate characters into custody. . . . It wasn't considered policy to draw a gun on Wyatt unless you got the drop and meant to burn powder without any preliminary talk." He stayed in Dodge City for most of July, and on July 21 a woman named Miss Frankie Bell received a slap from Wyatt. The *Dodge City Times* reported that Miss Bell "heaped epithets upon the unoffending head of Mr. Earp to such an extent as to provoke a slap from the ex-officer." She was put in jail for disturbing the peace and fined $20. Wyatt was assessed a fine of $1.

Wyatt left Dodge City in 1877 but returned in January 1878. According to Dodge City's *Ford County Globe*, Wyatt was in town on January 22 visiting from Fort Clark, Texas. On May 16, 1878, the *Wichita Eagle* reported, "Wyatt Earp, well known in this city, and for a long time connected with our police force, received an offer of $200 per month to take the Marshalship of Dodge City which he went up to accept, with all its dangers and responsibilities last week." Two days later he was listed in the paper as the assistant marshal to Charles Bassett. Dodge City was so happy with him that on June 27, 1878, the *Wichita Eagle* reported, "Wyatt is doing his duty as Assistant Marshal in a very credible manner. Adding new laurels to his splendid record every day." One of those laurels included putting out the flames of a fire that blazed four miles from town. By April 1879 Dodge City was touting itself as a prosperous town that did not rely solely on the Texas cattle trade. The *Dodge City Times* reported a story from a correspondent with the *Atchison Champion*. The unnamed reporter wrote:

Before going to Dodge I was told to stay away; that it was not safe to be on the streets after night; and that it was run by robbers, pick-pockets and rowdies. Just the reverse of this is true. I visited this town in November last, and formed the same impression of it then that I did to-day that it is as moral, quiet a business center as any town on the Atchison, Topeka & Santa Fe railroad. There had been a city election a day or two before, and I am assured there was less drunkenness and boisterous words used than in any town in Kansas. Her efficient police force are ever on the alert for roughs, and through their indefatigable efforts to preserve order, a person is no more liable to be knocked down and robbed here than he is in Atchison. The new city government is composed of the following gentlemen: Mayor, James H. Kelley . . . Marshal, C. E. Bassett; Deputy Marshal, Wyat [sic] Earp. . . . Dodge is not as lively now as it will be a month hence, or during the Texas cattle drive, which will commence about the middle of May. It is estimated that there will be more than 200,000 cattle drives into Dodge this season, or an increase of over 50,000 since last year.

Another evidence of the permanence of Dodge City is the fact that many elegant residences and large, commodious business houses are in course of construction at the present time. Looking through many of the business homes, and courting three and six in each, all busy, if indicative of good times, certainly Dodge cannot complain. "Dull times" is scarcely heard in Dodge; they are happy, good-natured and prosperous.

Despite this glowing report, Wyatt apparently felt this town was becoming much too sedate to hold his interest. Later in life he recalled, "In 1879 Dodge was beginning to lose much of the snap which had given it a charm to men of restless blood, and I decided to move to

Tombstone, which was just building up a reputation."[6] He also received a letter from his older brother Virgil telling him to come to Arizona and join him in the new boomtown of Tombstone.

Wyatt's third wife, Celia Ann "Mattie" Blaylock, is believed to have been with Wyatt in Dodge City—at least for a portion of his time there. Celia Ann went by a few names, but history remembers her as Mattie. She was the third of six children born to Henry and Elizabeth "Betsy" Blaylock. According to family records, Henry was born in Ohio around 1821. He married fourteen-year-old Elizabeth, with her parents' verbal consent, on July 20, 1841, in Boone County, Indiana. On January 11, 1849, he purchased land from Oliver Blaylock in Monroe Township, Iowa, and it was in this rural farm country where Henry and Betsy would raise their family.

Celia Ann came into the world on a cold Iowa day in January 1850. She had an older sister named Martha Jane and an older brother named Marion. Her younger siblings included Sarah Ellen, William, and Toni May. Celia Ann lost three of her siblings early on and her mother, Betsy, buried her husband and four of her six children before her own death in 1899. Celia Ann's older sister, Martha Blaylock-Probst, died in 1872; her brother Marion, who served in the Civil War, died of consumption in 1870; and her brother William died in 1876. Her father passed away on May 9, 1877, by which time Celia Ann had already left home.

Celia Ann's father was a farmer by trade near a small but up-and-coming town where she attended school with her siblings. When Celia Ann was nine, the town had 1,200 residents, six churches, and only one saloon. On April 14, 1869, the *Daily State Iowa Register* reported on the growing town of Monroe, Iowa: "Such a busy little town; such friendly people, and such pretty women . . . many new buildings are going up, and all together Monroe has a lively appearance." Celia Ann's parents, Betsy and Henry, were strict, traditional Lutherans who

Henry and Betsy Blaylock were the parents of Celia Ann "Mattie" Blaylock, who married Wyatt Earp. COURTESY ANCESTRY.COM

stood for no nonsense. No evidence exists as to how old Celia Ann and her younger sister Sarah were when they supposedly ran away. Celia Ann was at home when she was ten in 1860, but then does not appear again until she's in the 1880 Tombstone census. While Celia Ann never returned home, Sarah did and was eventually married, for a brief time. Celia Ann and her sisters would have been taught all the things little girls, who would one day become keepers of their own homes, learned. They learned to sew, cook, can fruits and vegetables, and be demure—after all, it was the Victorian era.

Six churches and one saloon were hardly considered lively by those who sought a faster-paced, exciting life. To Celia Ann, it must have seemed quite boring, and by the time the 1870 census was taken, she had left home. Just what Celia Ann did once she left Iowa is again left to speculation due to lack of evidence. Some of the acceptable jobs for a single woman back in the day included working in a hotel or restaurant, sewing, cleaning, and washing. Some women willingly turned to prostitution because they earned quick money and retired into a comfortable life. Others became prostitutes because they needed to eat. In 1871 Celia Ann, who adopted the name Mattie, was living in Fort Scott, Kansas, where she posed for a photograph. Since Wyatt was also in this area, it's possible this is where Mattie first met him.

Mattie and Wyatt called themselves husband and wife, but since no documentation has been discovered, there's no way to know whether their union was legal. In September 1879 Wyatt resigned in Dodge City and was headed to Las Vegas, New Mexico, and then went on to Prescott, Arizona, to meet his older brother Virgil.

Around the time they headed for Tombstone, Wyatt was working as a shotgun messenger for Wells Fargo. As he stopped over in Tucson in late 1879, Sheriff Shibell convinced him to become the deputy sheriff of Pima County. His brother Morgan succeeded him in his position with Wells Fargo.

When Mattie and Wyatt reached Tombstone the rich mineral deposits were already being mined, and the town's population swelled to some 5,300 residents in the summer of 1880. Tombstone's boom lasted longer than most mining towns' did, and Tombstone eventually became "family oriented," as residents became confident in their future. Tombstone was often compared to San Francisco when it came to sophistication, and its growing prosperity was giving rise to fraternal organizations, churches, numerous social events, upscale hotels, and elegant saloons.

This boomtown sat atop one of the most productive mining areas in the Southwest. Tombstone's mines peaked from mid-1879, when

Celia Ann "Mattie" Blaylock posed for this photo in 1871 in Fort Scott, Kansas. GLENN BOYER COLLECTION, COURTESY OF SCOTT DYKE

the Earps arrived, to late 1882. During this pinnacle, the mines produced on average over $5 million annually in silver and gold. The larger mining companies paid an average of $600,000 in dividends annually.

In addition to the breweries, wine rooms, saloons, and dance houses, other types of entertainment were available for hardworking men. The sources of entertainment covered the spectrum from sophisticated theater programs to rough and rowdy cockfights, and everything in between. In early September 1881, a dog race took place between Brook's "Bulldozer" and Earp's blue dog, "Jim." They ran two heats around the track, and Bulldozer was the victor. Tombstone boasted a racetrack, a bowling alley where James Earp worked, a skating rink, an in-ground swimming pool, baseball games, boxing matches, and more, which kept many a resident entertained in the liveliest silver mining camp Arizona has ever seen. Tombstone's number of saloons reflected the town's boom and Wyatt took advantage. By mid-1880, there were about twenty-six saloons and breweries, and by July of the following year, the number of saloons in Tombstone had doubled. The year 1881 was no doubt the best year for Tombstone's saloons, and the quantity of them was never higher.

Tombstone saloonkeepers entertained their customers with classical music, or tunes played by Tombstone's brass band, or an Italian string ensemble. Even though these saloons were more or less respectable, Tombstone's society women did not go into them because no respectable woman dared enter a saloon—it just was not proper. Not to mention that men did not want them there; this was a place where they could seek solace among their brethren. Alcohol and music aside, Tombstone's saloons also drew crowds because of the gambling.

Gambling concessions and cigar stands were nestled in the saloons, and were often run by someone other than the saloon owners. Most had a separate section for gambling, usually in the back. However, the reader should not envision that old Hollywood image of a secluded, smoke-filled room where a bunch of desperadoes were ready to kill one another over a hand of cards. It is true a gambler could get shot over a game of cards, but only if he were caught cheating. The most popular saloon games of the time were faro, monte, and poker, but other saloons offered keno, roulette, and twenty-one.

It was into this bustling, noisy mining town that Mattie, who was now calling herself Mrs. Earp, followed her husband and his brothers. Mattie and Wyatt, along with Virgil and his wife, Allie; James and his wife, Bessie; and Bessie's daughter, Hattie, arrived in Tombstone, Arizona, in late 1879. After Mattie and Wyatt arrived, they found small homes to live in and Wyatt and his brothers set out to earn a living. Wyatt served as deputy sheriff from October 1879 until 1880. On July 29, 1880, the *Daily Epitaph* wrote, "Wyatt has filled various positions in which bravery and determination were requisites, and in every instance proved himself the right man in the right place." The brothers filed mining claims in the bustling silver mining town they now called home and Wyatt even named one "The Mattie Blaylock." On November 13, 1880, Wyatt, Virgil, and James Earp, along with Robert J. Winders, applied for a patent to the 1st North Extension of the Mountain Maid mine. The mine had a twenty-six-foot-long shaft and had three buildings, each about fourteen feet by thirty-four feet in size. This mine bordered the Yreka, Mattie Blaylock, and Lala Rook claims.

Wyatt eventually secured an interest in a gambling concession at the Oriental Saloon, where he spent many a night. Mattie, on the other hand, was left to stay at home with the other Earp wives. They cooked, visited, wrote letters, read the local papers, sewed, and kept house. Mattie reportedly suffered from severe gum disease and headaches and, as a result, became addicted to laudanum, which was a liquid tincture made from opium. It's not known when this addiction began, but she is known to have used laudanum in Tombstone. Despite her

Fly's Gallery,   Tombstone, A. T.

This photo has no identification, but was taken in Tombstone by well-known photographer Camillus S. Fly about the time Mattie Earp lived there (1879–1882) and bears a striking resemblance to her other photos, although there is no confirmation that this is Mattie. COURTESY OF ROBERT G. MCCUBBIN

health issues, she and Virgil's wife, Allie, put their sewing skills to use and earned a penny per yard they sewed for the local townspeople.

Mattie and Allie weren't just sisters-in-law, they were also close friends. The two were known to act like schoolgirls sometimes. One hot summer day Mattie and Allie ventured into town because they grew tired of sitting in their homes and wanted to see the luxurious hotels and fancy restaurants. They met a "friend" who treated them to samples of very nice wine, which the ladies enjoyed—a bit too much. When they got home, they went straight to bed, hoping to avoid being found out by their husbands, but Wyatt and Virgil came home unexpectedly. Virgil just stared at Allie while Wyatt tried to get Mattie to drink coffee without spilling it all over. Allie fondly recalled, "Mattie was as fine a woman as ever lived. . . . Stuck with him through thick and thin. And was there every minute. Someday," Allie added mysteriously, "I'll tell you why she doesn't even get her name mentioned as bein' alive."

At some point in 1881, Wyatt became enamored of another woman in Tombstone. Josephine Sarah Marcus had been in Tombstone as the fiancée of Cochise County marshal (and Wyatt's soon-to-be nemesis) Johnny Behan. Johnny was a womanizer and strayed on Josephine, so she left him. No one from that time period really mentioned the affair between Wyatt and Josephine, but then again, it was the Victorian era and people rarely put those things in print. Those details were often left for private gossiping. Regardless, Mattie stayed in Tombstone, even while Wyatt was seeing Josephine. It's not known whether Mattie was aware of the affair. Either she knew about it and had nowhere else to go, was determined to stick with Wyatt despite his cheating, or simply had no clue.

She went about her life, reading, sewing, and visiting with her sisters-in-law. She took laudanum for the pain she endured, and her drug-induced brain drifted into oblivion. Most drugs of the Victorian era contained large amounts of alcohol or an addictive drug like opium. Mattie was not the only woman of her time to become an addict. It happened more frequently than most people realize.

Despite what was going on around her, Mattie stayed in Tombstone, and was there during the gunfight on October 26, 1881. Her husband was the only one of the Earp brothers who was not injured in the fight, and Mattie must have been relieved when Wyatt came home. According to her sister-in-law Allie, when Mattie heard the gunshots down the street, she wanted to go to Wyatt to see what happened, but her hair was in curlers and she was too embarrassed to show herself in public, like any Victorian lady of the day would have felt. It was likely a surprise for Mattie and all the other Earp wives when they learned their husbands were involved in the fight. Women of that time were rarely included in conversations about politics or other male-dominated affairs. It's also unlikely Wyatt would have talked to Mattie about town matters or possible trouble brewing—even if she was coherent.

Shortly after the attempt on Virgil's life in December 1881 all the Earps, including Mattie, moved into the Cosmopolitan Hotel for safety reasons. It's assumed Mattie did not leave Tombstone until after the death of Morgan on March 18, 1882, but on February 22, 1882, Mattie Earp is shown as a new arrival at the Cosmopolitan, where she stated she was from Cedar Rapids, Iowa. Although most of Mattie's Iowa family members had passed away by this time, this record indicates that she may have visited Iowa while the rest of the Earps were staying at the Cosmopolitan.

Mattie must have been Wyatt's legal partner—or at least that's what they told people—because in early 1882, she and Wyatt mortgaged their adobe home for $365 at 2 percent interest. This was right around the time when the inquest was being held for the gunfight near the OK Corral. Despite the perception of Victorian women not being independent, some owned property jointly with their spouses or independently. Others even owned businesses in frontier towns, such as restaurants, bakeries, millinery shops, saloons, and dance halls.

On March 24, 1882, Mattie, along with James's wife, Bessie, left for their husbands' parents' home in Colton, California, after Morgan's tragic death in March. The following day they arrived in Los Angeles and the *Los Angeles Herald* noted, "Mrs. J.C. Earp and Mrs. Wyatt Earp, of Tombstone" were arriving at 4:45 p.m. Mattie's husband stayed on to avenge his brother's death.

Mattie waited for her husband to return to her at his parents' home in Colton. Sometime in late 1882 Wyatt did head to California, but he went to San Francisco and moved in with Virgil and Warren, who lived at 604 Pine Street. It's interesting to note the fourth Mrs. Wyatt Earp, Josephine Marcus, also was living in San Francisco by that time. Wyatt had chosen his mistress over his wife. Mattie's sister-in-law Allie recalled Mattie and Wyatt having a fight, but she never alluded to what it was about or when. By April 1883 Wyatt was officially traveling with Josephine.

With her husband brazenly parading around with another woman as his wife, Mattie headed back to Arizona around August 1882. She settled in Globe for a while and by 1885 she was living in Pinal, Arizona, which was a silver, gold, and copper mining community. Wyatt's rejection and her health issues had turned Mattie into a woman who lived in an alcohol- and drug-induced state most of her days. On July 3, 1888, she committed suicide. On July 14, the Globe *Arizona Silverbelt* ran this notice: "Mattie Earp, who formerly lived in Globe, committed suicide in Pinal on Tuesday of last week, by taking laudanum. The *Enterprise* states that she had been on a protracted spree."

Her death inquisition tells of a sad, tragic end to Mattie's life:

Inquisition—Mattie Earp—Deceased
Filed July 21, 1888
W. Wood Porter, Clerk

In the matter of the inquisition held upon the body of Mattie Earp deceased.
The following named witnesses were sworn and testified as follows:

Frank Beuler duly sworn on his oath says:

Q. What is your name, age, occupation and residence?

A. My name is Frank Beuler. I am 65 years of age. I am a laborer and live in Pinal, Ariz.

Q. State to the jury all that you know about the cause of the death of the deceased.

A. The woman felt sick and I knew pretty well what the sickness was as I had waited on her once before when she was the same way. I went to her room here in Pinal day before yesterday and looked in the door. I asked her if she wanted anything as I was in the habit of doing some chores for her. She said no she didn't want anything. She was lying on the bed and a man was lying there on the bed beside of her. During that day I didn't go there again but yesterday I went there about 8 or 9 o'clock in the morning she was lying on the bed and I asked her if she wanted anything and she said come in here and sit down I want to talk to you. I went in and sat down and she said she didn't feel well and pointed around beside the stand to a beer bottle that stood there. I took the bottle and it contained whiskey about one fourth full and she and I drank it up. She said then that she wanted to get more whiskey and some opium or Laudanum as she wanted to try and get some sleep. While she was lying there I said where are your bracelets and she said I guess they are around here somewhere. I couldn't find them but found her small breastpin. I put it up on the wall. She then said I would like to have you go to Luedke's and get me some Laudanum as I cannot sleep. She then said go to Werners and get more whiskey. I went there and got fifty cents worth of whiskey and took it to her. Then she wanted me to go and get her Laudanum. I went to Luedke and he gave me a small bottle of Laudanum and I took it to her. I asked Leudke how much of that to make them sleep and he said he didn't know but that she had been taking it for a long time. Then I went back with the Laudanum. I said I didn't know how much a dose is and she said give me about twenty drops. I counted out about fifteen drops and said how much whiskey do you want in it and hold the glass up and pour it out and she said when I had enough. She then took it and drank it. She then said come and sit down and talk and I said how do you feel and she said better and that she thought she could sleep. I sat there about an hour and then went in the other room as I was feeling the liquor. I laid down and about that time Flannery came to the door and I then went out and I was gone about two hours when I went back to her house and as I wanted a drink I looked around for the whiskey but couldn't find any and the whole bottle of Laudanum was gone. I felt of her pulse and her heart and they seemed to be beating allright and she seemed to be asleep. I sat down then for an hour or two and then went out as I thought she was asleep. I was away about two hours and then went back and saw a number of persons in there. The Dr. [Kenaird] was one of them and seemed to be trying to restore her. The Dr. asked me if there was any whiskey there.

Q. What time of day did you get the Laudanum from Luedke?

A. I cannot tell but it was in the forenoon and I gave it to her right away.

Q. What time was it when you went back there last and found the Dr. there?

A. It must have been four or five o'clock.

Q. Were you sober during the day yesterday?

A. I can't say that I was. Though I was able to attend to business.

Q. Wasn't you pretty drunk in the afternoon?

A. I was but I didn't give her any Laudanum when I was drunk.

Q. What did you do with the bottle after giving her the Laudanum?

A. I sat it up on the shelf.

Q. Was she up during the day?

A. Yes.

Q. Why did you feel her pulse when you went in?

A. Because I saw the Laudanum was gone.

Q. Was there Laudanum enough in the bottle to have killed any person if they had taken it all in your opinion?

A. I don't know how much it takes. I don't think I gave her an eighth of what was in the bottle.

(s) F Beuler

Subscribed & sworn to before me this 4th day of July A.D. 1888. W. H. Benson, Acting Comm. Pinal County, Arizona.

T. J. Flannery being duly sworn on his oath says:

Q. What is your name, age, occupation and residence?

A. My name is T. J. Flannery. I am 31 years of age. I reside in Pinal, Ariz. occupation laborer.

Q. State to the jury all that you [know] about the cause of the death of the deceased.

A. I went to her room here in Pinal last night about eight o'clock or a little after and knocked on the door but no one answered. I hadn't seen her since Sunday or Monday. The door was opened very soon by Beuler who said that the deceased was lying on the bed asleep. I went in and saw by the position that she was lying in that something was wrong as she would not be that way unless something was wrong. I lit a light and went up to the bed and looked at her and her arms and face were covered with black spots. I supposed she had been taking more Laudanum and had taken too much and was dead or dying. I felt of her pulse and found the heart not beating. I asked Beuler what she had been taking and he said he gave her some Laudanum and that she had taken the whiskey bottle. I then started out for the Dr. and met him as he was going home. He went in and tried to restore the deceased but couldn't do so. It was about half past eight when the Dr. got there.

Q. What condition was Beuler in when he came to the door to let you in?

A. I didn't pay much attention to him. I do not think he was drunk.

Q. What is the name of the deceased if you know?

A. Mattie Earp

(s) T. J. Flannery

T. J. Flannery recalled.

Q. Did you ever hear the deceased threaten her own life?

A. I have. Earp she said had wrecked her life by deserting her and she didn't want to live.

(s) T. J. Flannery

Subscribed & sworn to before me on this 4th day of July A.D. 1888. W. H. Benson, Acting Comm.

S. E. Damon being duly sworn on his oath says:

Q. What is your name, age, occupation and residence?

A. My name is S. E. Damon. I am 31 years of age, occupation Laborer and I live in Pinal Ariz.

Q. State to the jury all that you know about the cause of death of the deceased.

A. I do not know anything about the cause of the death. I know what she has been drinking heavily for about three months and I have several times taken whiskey away from her. About three days ago she said she was going to make away with herself as she said she was tired of life.

(s) S. E. Damon

Subscribed and sworn to before me this 4th day of July A.D. 1888. W. H. Benson, Acting Comm. Pinal County Ariz.

I hereby certify that the above and foregoing are true and correct depositions taken by me in the inquisition upon the body of Mattie Earp, deceased, held July 4th 1888.

(s) W. H. Benson

*Acting Comm. Pinal,
Pinal Co., Arizona*[7]

Celia Ann Blaylock, who became Mattie Earp, died sad, abandoned, and alone.

Mattie Blaylock Earp kept the name Earp even after Wyatt left her for Josephine. COURTESY OF ROBERT G. MCCUBBIN

When Wyatt finished avenging his brother's cold-blooded murder, he headed to San Francisco, where he met up with his fourth and final wife, Josephine Sarah "Sadie" Marcus. Throughout her entire life, from birth to death, Josephine was a woman of secrets and mystery. Since no records exist to prove her birth, detective work was needed to create an estimation. It appears she was born on June 2, 1861, to Hyman "Henry" Marcus and Sophie Lewis-Levy, but no records could be located for anyone in the Marcus family in the 1860 US census or the New York census. It's possible no records exist because many New York pre–Civil War birth records are missing, and it's impossible to know if this is her exact birth date. What is known is that on July 11, 1870, she was recorded as being nine years old when the US census was taken. One of her parents would have given her age to the census taker, so it's pretty likely the 1861 birth date is accurate. Also, the birth year on her tombstone is 1861. It's especially curious that Josephine claims to not have known her own birth date, especially considering that her sister Hattie threw her a sixty-fifth birthday party on June 2, 1925.[8] Using the birthday party date, that puts the date of her birth on June 2, 1860—off by one year. Since it's customary to host parties on weekends, the fact that Josephine's sixty-fifth birthday was celebrated on a Tuesday would lead to the assumption that June 2 was her actual birthday. From the 1870 census through the 1880 census, Josephine's birth year remains the same, which is 1861. Beginning in 1900, she began to vary her age and birth date from 1861 to 1869 when each census was taken.

In 1942, just two years before her death, Josephine curiously sent a letter to the New York City Department of Health asking if they had a record of her birth. People have been keeping records of births and deaths in Bibles for years, and most knew their dates, so it's odd that Josephine did such a thing. One has to wonder whether Josephine might have been adopted and was trying to find out the names of her birth parents, or if she was trying to discover some other details.

Hyman Henry Marcus was born in Poland in 1836 into an Eastern European Jewish family living in Nakel, Posen. Being an Eastern European Jew was far different from being a proper German Jew—Polish Jews were looked down upon by the German Jews and they did not travel in the same social circles. Hyman was a baker by trade who arrived in New York City in 1853, possibly on board the *Hammonia*. Even though he was a baker, the ship's manifest listed him as a tailor. But then again, the other twelve men listed above him were tailors as well. He married Sophie Lewis-Levy, who was born August 8, 1828.

Sophie, like her daughter, is elusive about her heritage—at least on her paper trail for a searching genealogist. She had been previously married and had a daughter named Rebecca Levy, who was born in St. Louis, Missouri, in September 1852.[9] At some point Sophie must have traveled back to New York City, where she met Hyman and gave birth to Nathan in 1857, and then later had Josephine, followed by Henrietta "Hattie." On the 1870 census, Sophie claimed she was born in Denmark, but in the 1880 census she said she was born in Prussia. Then in 1900 she stated she was from Germany. It's also curious that on her 1900 census she claimed to be the mother of six children, of which four were still living. However, to add to this confusing puzzle, Sophie is documented in the 1910 census as having emigrated from Germany to the United States in 1861, and was the mother of four children, of which three were still living—however, she was eighty-one at the time. An 1861 arrival seems unlikely since Rebecca stated in every census since 1870 that she was born in Missouri and her parents were both from Germany. In the 1920 census Rebecca stated they were both born in Berlin, while in the same year Josephine claimed their birthplace was Hamburg.

Regardless of when Josephine's parents married, there is a clue as to where they lived in an 1866 New York City tax record where a Henry Marcuse is listed as a manufacturer, which could have meant baker. He lived at 92 Hester Street, which was where other Jewish newcomers lived. Since there is no match for Henry Marcuse in the 1870 New York City census, it's fairly likely this was Josephine's father, since the Marcus family had moved to California by then. It was here on Hester Street where pushcarts and storefronts with awnings lined the streets in the Lower East Side. Today it's recognized as a Jewish cultural landmark due to its significance to the early Jewish immigrants in New York.

By the time the 1870 census was taken, Josephine and her family were living in San Francisco, where she and her siblings attended school. Hyman Marcuse is listed in the *Pacific Coast Business Directory* for 1871 as a baker working for Julius Dobrzensky at the Overland Bakery at 1218 Powell Street. Marcuse's residence was listed as 550 Clara Street. Dobrzensky's bakery must have failed, because the following year he was working as a gas meter taker at Union Brass, which his brother owned, and Josephine's father is listed as a peddler, possibly of baked goods. From 1872 until 1875 Josephine's father was listed as Henry Marcus in the directories. His name varied between Marcus and Marcuse almost as often as the family moved.

In 1870 the Marcus family resided at 1211 Powell Street and Josephine attended the Powell Street Primary School, which sat between Jackson and Washington Streets. There were 482 pupils enrolled with about 55 students per teacher. A historical sketch was written in 1879, which described the school as "a two-story building, containing eight small and poorly arranged rooms . . . this is probably the oldest American school building in San Francisco, being erected by the Rev. F. E. Preveaux, for a private school in 1850. The first public school was opened in the building on the 14th of June, 1855. It was first organized as Grammar School, but June 10th, 1861 the Grammar pupils with their Principal and teachers, were transferred to the Washington Grammar School, when it was re-organized as a Primary School."

Josephine once told her biographers, "In the schools of old San Francisco one saw the inconsistency of a tolerant and gay population acting as merciless and self-righteous as a New England village in bringing up its children." Her teachers included Misses L.W. Burwell, S. S. Knapp, L. A. Winn, Sarah E. Thurton, Mrs. Eliza S. Forester, and Misses Mary E. Tucker, Eliza Damez, and Margery Robertson. Her principal, Miss Carrie V. Benjamin, was a twenty-five-year-old native of Pennsylvania.[10] Benjamin had been a teacher and a principal at various schools in San Francisco as early as 1863 when she was at the Rincon Grammar School. She became principal at Josephine's Powell Street school in 1866.[11] Carrie married Charles Gummer in 1873, became a mother of one, and left the school system. By 1900, she was an unemployed widow living at a boardinghouse on Pine Street.

Josephine didn't like Miss Benjamin very much and her biographers recalled, "To the end of her days Josie was to sneak out and feed every stray cat or dog in whatever neighborhood she should find herself. Once, while worrying about a little white dog, she excused herself so frequently that her teacher finally realized that her absences were not of a legitimate nature. Up she went to the principal's office. Mrs. Benjamin sighed as she tiptoed into her room, frozen with fright, wide, dark eyes distended. 'You here again, Josephine! What now?' Through her tears she tried to explain, but Mrs. Benjamin would not understand. After listening impatiently she commanded, 'Hold out your hands, palms up!'" She would then be slapped for punishment.[12] She was no doubt thrilled to leave Carrie Benjamin's school when in 1871 the Marcuses moved to 550 Clara Street where she attended the primary school at Fourth and Clara Streets. In 1870 a new teacher named Miss Emma Stinson was installed at the school. In 1871 the school had approximately 534 pupils, of which 95 percent regularly attended. Monthly tuition was $1.56. An 1879 historical sketch read, "This school is located at the corner of Fourth and Clara streets, in a frail and poorly arranged wooden building, containing ten small class-rooms. This was originally the old Rincon Grammar building on Hampton Place, and was removed to the present location in 1863. The school also occupies a rented building, containing six rooms, on the corner of Mission and Mary streets. It is a mixed school for boys and girls, and contains about eight hundred and eighty pupils. It was opened in April, 1863 under the supervision of Mr. A. E. McGlynn. Mr. McGlynn was succeeded by Mrs. L. A. Morgan, who was elected in 1865 and remained until April 18, 1876, when she tendered her resignation." Even though the Marcuses moved again, it was only a block over. Josephine probably continued her education at the same school when they moved over to 102 Shipley Street in 1872 and then to 221 Clara Street in 1874.

In addition to traditional school, Josephine attended a dancing academy and told her biographers, "Hattie and I attended the McCarthy Dancing Academy for children on Howard Street. Eugenia and Lottie McCarthy taught us to dance the Highland Fling, the Sailor's Hornpipe, and ballroom dancing."[13] Josephine's account of this is almost correct. There was a dancing academy run by the McCarty family, which included a team of brothers and sisters. Between 1870 and 1874 Dennis Samuel, Eugene, Lottie, and Nellie gave lessons. However, none of the business directories list them at Howard Street. They are always listed at 139 Post Street, which would have been a fifteen-minute walk for Josephine and Hattie from their Powell Street home. It would have been a twenty-minute walk from Clara Street, where they moved next. There was a Eugene McCarty who was a ship painter and lived on Howard, but it's not known whether he was the Eugene associated with the academy. In January 1870 the McCartys advertised in the *San Francisco Bulletin,* "FOUR PRACTICAL TEACHERS. D. McCarty, E. McCarty, Miss Lotta McCarty, Miss Nellie McCarty. New Dancing Academy, No. 21 Montgomery Street, opposite Lick House. New classes now forming. Pupils taught correctly in all the fashionable dances, deportment, etc. and in half the usual time, as the teachers practice individually with all pupils. Call and get circular. Soirees Saturday evening at 5 ½ o'clock." The following month they relocated to Post Street. On May 1, 1873, the McCarty Dancing Academy had a performance at the Children's May Festival where their students gave dance performances to honor May Day. An open-air performance by a local band named Krauss's accompanied the dancers. In late 1874 brothers Dennis and Eugene were arrested for assaulting a pupil, but the newspaper account included, "It is understood the alleged assault was a trivial affair and in no way warranted such an arbitrary procedure."

As the economy shifted, Josephine's father could no longer provide for his family, and around 1878 they all moved in with Josephine's half-sister, Rebecca, and her husband, Aaron Weiner, at 138 Perry Street. Josephine often told people she was rich and her family lived in well-to-do neighborhoods where other Jewish families lived, but that was not the case.[14] By 1882 Josephine's family had moved to 720 McAllister Street and again lived with her half-sister Rebecca Weiner at least until 1895, when their mother, Sophie, died.[15]

This is where the documentable facts on Josephine end until the late 1800s. Much has been written about Josephine's life in San Francisco and how she ended up in Arizona, and most of it was based on Josephine's recollections. However, with access to more records than ever before, historians and others have begun to find flaws in Josephine's tales of her life. How could she know that one day researchers would be able to fact-check her story with the click of a button? In her stories, events she recalled do not match, people are in places where they truly were not, and the timing of many things is just not possible.

She was quite dodgy about much of her life between 1870 and 1885, especially regarding her relationship with her fiancé Johnny Behan. Her early relationship with Wyatt Earp was another area she kept quite secret. When one compares the possibility of her recollections by verifying names, dates, and places, Josephine's memories seem to have faded, become embellished, or both.

Let's begin with her remembrance of her friend Dora Hirsch, with whom she was supposed to have run away in 1879 to join Pauline Markham's troupe, which was performing Gilbert & Sullivan's comedy/operetta *HMS Pinafore*. In 1870 Josephine was ten years old and claimed she and Dora took music lessons from Dora's mother. No records could be found in San Francisco for a *Dora* Hirsch in the 1870 census, but there was a Hirsch family living right next door to the Marcus family. Unfortunately for Josephine, the only woman at that house was forty-five-year-old Emily, who was keeping house. Her husband was a cigar packer and she had two sons. So just who was Dora, if she even existed?

There was a young woman named Leah Hirschberg, two years younger than Josephine, whose mother, Betsy, began to publicly offer music lessons beginning in 1874 after her husband died. It's also likely she offered them from her home earlier than that, as Josephine mentioned. It's quite possible this is the family to which Josephine was referring, but changed the names to hide their true identities so her story couldn't be verified. Betsy also owned a confectionary at 406 Third Street. Leah's father was also a baker who worked from his home, so maybe he and Hyman worked together. By 1882 Leah had taken over giving music lessons. The Hirschbergs lived around the corner from Josephine's sister, Rebecca Weiner, during most of the 1870s. When Betsy Hirschberg married her second husband, Otto Katz, in 1879, she and Leah and two younger siblings moved to 103 Perry Street. Josephine and her family were living at 138 Perry Street.

If the first part of Josephine's story begins with an untruth, how can the rest of her story be completely believed? Clearly Josephine needed to have information from which she told her story. It makes complete sense she used what was around her—even if she didn't experience it. Her friend Leah Hirschberg enjoyed a brief stint as a juvenile actress in San Francisco.[16] After Josephine returned from Arizona, she was ill and needed bed rest. Since Leah lived down the street, she likely visited her friend and regaled her with stories of her acting career. Josephine was eighty years old and slightly senile when she told her life story, but she still managed to interweave fact with fiction.

According to Josephine, she and Dora ran away from home in 1879. However, if she left home in 1879, she would have been eighteen, so running away hardly would have been necessary since she was an adult. She also noted, "I left my home one morning, carrying my books just as though I was going to school as usual." An eighteen-year-old woman would not be pretending to go to school. Another problem with this story is that she mentions they left to join the *HMS Pinafore* troupe, headed to Arizona. Nowhere is there documented proof that shows Josephine Marcus was with Pauline Markham's troupe. It is true actors often took stage names, but why didn't Josephine mention that? There is a reference in a 1966 newsletter called the *Smoke Signal*, in which author Pat Ryan wrote, "'Miss May Bell,' who played cousin Hebe in *Pinafore*, is nowadays well-known to Tombstone folklorists by her real name, Josephine Sarah Marcus. Wyatt Earp and Johnny Behan are said to have vied for her favors during the brief Tombstone stand." Ryan does not, however, cite any reference for that information. The October 21, 1879, edition of the *Los Angeles Herald* named the members of the *Pinafore* troupe en route to Tucson and May Bell was one of the actresses named. However, the only May Bell listed as an actress in *Langley's San Francisco City Directory, 1879,* was living on Sixteenth Street, so it's not likely this was Josephine.

As for Josephine's account of traveling to Arizona, there is again inconsistency. If in fact she traveled with Pauline Markham's troupe, she would not have taken a stagecoach from California, as she claimed. Markham's troupe took the train to the end of the tracks at Casa Grande, Arizona, sixty-five miles northwest of Tucson, and then traveled the last leg by stagecoach. The route that Josephine described, in which she stated she traveled from Los Angeles to Arizona, crossing into Arizona by ferry at Ehrenberg, was the route to Prescott, not the route to Tucson, where the troupe made its first stop. If Josephine took the route she claimed, then she was neither with Pauline Markham nor headed to Tucson.

On October 25, 1879, the Yuma *Arizona Sentinel* reported, "Tuesday arrived a *Pinafore* Company for Tucson, composed of Misses Pauline Markham, Mary Bell, Belle Howard and Mrs. Pring, and Messrs. Borabeck and McMahon. Tucson has our condolences." Just below that story they reported that Mr. McMahon with the *Pinafore* troupe declared he would expose the abominable way in which the passengers of the Southern Pacific Railroad had been treated. After Tucson, they went to Tombstone in early December, and then headed for Prescott. Pauline Markham arrived in Prescott, Arizona, in time to perform on Christmas Eve in 1879. She arrived with two members of the cast, and five others arrived two days later.[17]

It's also been speculated by some writers and historians that Josephine may have taken on a different persona when she ran away. So if Josephine did not go to Arizona with Pauline Markham's troupe in 1879, how and when did she get there?

If Josephine did in fact create a guise to run away, she might have been motivated to do so by her life in a lower-class Prussian family. If she'd stayed the course in San Francisco, she probably would have married a nice Jewish gentleman of her own class, had children, and lived a quiet, predictable life. However, based on Josephine's runaway tale, she wanted anything but that. So how does a poor girl get ahead and find the excitement she so desires? It appears in Josephine's case, she may have signed on with a nearby madam named Hattie Wells about 1874. Josephine's school was only one block from Hattie's establishment. It's possible the fourteen-year-old Josephine saw these women, nicely dressed and seemingly living a life of leisure, at least from the outside, and considered their occupation her ticket to the exciting life she craved. It was not uncommon for women—even free-spirited teenagers—to choose to be prostitutes to get what they wanted. These women were not your typical soiled doves, but more like high-class call girls who chose their customers and charged a tidy sum. Some madams actively recruited girls and women for their wealthy clientele. In 1870 Hattie, who also was from New York, had five women between the ages of seventeen and thirty working for her, and all her neighbors ran brothels as well.

Now, Hattie and her girls were in the 1000 block of Clay Street, a district known for prostitutes, and Josephine would have walked right past her establishment on her way to and from school. Did Hattie use less than scrupulous tactics to woo Josephine and other young girls? It's possible Hattie told the young girls they would have nice dresses, travel to exciting places, dine in fancy restaurants, and meet handsome men. Many young girls of the day may have believed her and got more than they bargained for—but they may also have known what they were getting into. Josephine later recalled these details to one of her biographers: "The whole experience recurs to my memory as a bad dream and I remember little of its details. I can remember shedding tears in out-of-the-way corners. I thought constantly of my mother and how great must be her grief and worry over me. In my confusion, I could see no way out of the tragic mess."[18]

Whether Josephine willingly joined Hattie or was duped, it appears she left with the madam and some other new recruits in 1874—making

Josephine just fourteen when they headed to Prescott. When she dictated her memoirs in later years, Josephine recalled how she and her best friend, Dora Hirsch, ran away with Pauline Markham's *Pinafore* troupe: "I kissed my mother good-by [*sic*] as usual, but instead of going to school, I went to my friend's house. The door opened before I knocked. Dora was fully dressed, waiting for me, and ready to go."[19]

The October 20, 1874, issue of the Prescott, Arizona, *Weekly Miner Journal* carried the following item: "Special Dispatches of the Arizona Miner by Western Union and US Military Lines. Named passengers who left Wickenberg this morning en route to Prescott from San Francisco: Miss Hattie Wells, Miss Ella Howard, Miss Saddie [*sic*] Mansfield, Miss Minnie Alice and Mrs. Julia Burton, a servant." It seems the girl named Josephine Marcus "stayed" in San Francisco as her alter ego Sadie Mansfield headed to Arizona.

It's interesting to note the 1870 census showed a Miss Ella Howard, who was ten years old, living with a music teacher named Joseph Rhind at Rincon Home in San Francisco. By 1874 Prescott's population was predominantly male as soldiers and miners flocked to the area. According to writer and researcher Roger Jay, "Among Hattie's entourage, was Ella Howard who already resided in Prescott the previous year.[20] Also in the traveling party from San Francisco, Mrs. Julia Burton can be traced through entries both in the 1870 and the 1880 US Census, where her race is given as 'mulatto.'"[21] This lends strong credence to Josephine's recollection of the Markham troupe in which she said, "I was soon caught in the midst of a chattering group of girls who awed me considerably—they were so 'stylish' and sophisticated. We piled in hacks and were driven down to the wharf where we boarded a steamer for Santa Barbara. A kind-faced NEGRESS was in the hack with us. She wore a beautiful paisley shawl. 'That's Aunt Julia—Miss Markham's maid,' one of the girls informed us."[22] What are the odds of both Pauline Markham's troupe and Hattie's entourage traveling with a black woman named Julia? This "recollection" is yet another example of how easily Josephine mixed fact and fiction throughout the story of her life.

It's a known fact Josephine fell for her first love, John "Johnny" Harris Behan, while she was traveling to Arizona. If she was with Hattie on her way to Prescott, it's likely she met Johnny then, since Prescott was in Yavapai County, where Behan was very active in the county legislature in 1873 and was well-known about town. He even ran for sheriff in late 1874. On October 6, 1874, the *Prescott Miner* reported, "J.H. Behan left on an 'electioneering' tour toward Black Canyon, Wickenburg and other places." He returned November 11, so Josephine could have met him while he was out touring. She recalled, "I can now speak casually of meeting one of them. He was young and darkly handsome, with merry black eyes and an engaging smile. My heart was stirred by his attentions in what were very romantic circumstances. It was a diversion from my homesickness though I cannot say I was in love with him. I was in a state of too great confusion to allow for any such deep feeling. His name was Johnny Behan. I do not know how he happened to be in that place at that time though I am under the impression that he was a deputy sheriff engaged on some official errand. This affair unimportant as it appears was to have a far-reaching effect upon my life."

On the surface Johnny appeared to be an upstanding citizen in his community. He was married to Victoria and was the father of Albert and Henrietta—although during his divorce, Johnny claimed Henrietta was not his. Josephine's new flame had a darker side, and was known to visit brothels. By December 1874 Sadie Mansfield was working in a brothel located on Granite Street, which was not far from the Yavapai County courthouse and the rooms where the Arizona territorial legislature used to meet.

In February Sadie Mansfield was charged with petty larceny for stealing some German tablespoons from a local store. Could this have been the fourteen-year-old Josephine's way of attempting to get enough money to return home and escape her tragic mess? Josephine remained in Prescott until at least the week of April 16, 1875, when she collected two letters being held for her at the post office.[23] She claimed scout Al Sieber was instrumental in getting her home. He did frequent Prescott and may have taken pity on her, but Sieber was based out of the Prescott area at Camp Verde only from 1873 to 1875. Per Josephine, Sieber contacted her brother-in-law Aaron Wiener, who was waiting for her in California. She told her biographers, "My frantic family had been uncovering every clue they could find as to my whereabouts but without success until Al Sieber, guessing my situation, got in touch with my brother-in-law, whose address I gave him, by military telegraph. My brother-in-law remembered a friend who lived in Prescott, Arizona, and he appealed to him at once, also using the military telegraph which was the only means of communication by wire at that time in Arizona." By March 1876 she had made it home, because she recalled being there to attend the opening of Lucky Baldwin's theater.[24]

Once she returned to San Francisco she recalled, "The fear and excitement, the weeks of exhausting travel, chagrin over my own foolishness, all together proved too much for my strength. I developed St. Vitus Dance and was unable to attend school very much again. After a time however I gradually improved in health so that within two years after my experience I was once more a normal healthy girl." Again, if Josephine was eighteen as she claimed, it is unclear why she would mention she couldn't attend school very much, and call herself a girl.

St. Vitus Dance is an acute, self-limited movement disorder that occurs most commonly in children between the ages of five and fifteen, and occasionally in pregnant women. It's characterized by rapid, uncoordinated jerking movements of the body.[25] St. Vitus Dance is a form of streptococcus, as is cerebrospinal meningitis. According to the *Journal of Pediatrics,* scarlet fever can lead to both St. Vitus Dance and meningitis. Both are contracted through saliva. It's interesting to note that both of Johnny's children, Henrietta and Albert, suffered from meningitis as early as 1877. In July 1877, eight-year-old Henrietta died from her illness. There were also a few cases of scarlet fever in Prescott as early as 1877. While the symptoms are somewhat different, both diseases come from the same strain of bacteria.

Johnny's infidelity resulted in a divorce request from his wife, Victoria, in May 1875. Charles Goodman served as her witness and testified, "I saw the defendant [Behan] at a house of ill fame . . . at which resided one Sada Mansfield, commonly called Sada, a woman of prostitution and ill-fame, and the said defendant did at the time and at the house spoken of, stay all night with and sleep with the said Sada Mansfield, and I know of the defendant having committed similar acts at the same place and at various times other than at the particular time above referred to."[26] [27]

When Josephine did finally return home, she said her family explained "her escapades" and absence by simply telling anyone outside the immediate family that she had been away on a visit. Josephine said of that time, "The memory of it has been a source of humiliation and regret to me all the years since that time and I have never until now disclosed it to anyone besides my husband."[28]

In March 1879, Johnny Behan's son, Albert, was experiencing some deafness and was taken to San Francisco for treatment. Josephine stated Johnny had come to San Francisco to propose marriage. She turned him down at first but then agreed, saying, "Life was dull for me in San Francisco. In spite of my sad experience of a few years ago the call to adventure *still* stirred my blood."[29] This remark reveals yet another inconsistency in Josephine's tangled life story, making her travels with Pauline Markham's troupe even less likely: If she had been in Tombstone with Markham in 1879, it's unclear why she would say "a few years ago."

Johnny and Albert were back in Phoenix as early as May 1879. In October the *Weekly Journal Miner* noted Johnny was going to open a business in the silver mining community of Tip Top, Arizona, near Gillette. Both were in Yavapai County, and Gillette was the mill town where the silver from the Tip Top mines was melted down—today they're ghost towns. Johnny's saloon was in the old Martin Saffenburg building. The town had six saloons, but only five prostitutes to service a booming mining community. Sadie Mansfield followed Johnny Behan to Tip Top. The June 2, 1880, US census listed her as a "Courtesan," age nineteen, born in New York of German parentage. Now, Josephine Marcus is also enumerated on the same day in San Francisco as living with her parents, which prevents the Sadie Mansfield guise from being a solid case. However, Josephine herself said her parents hid her activities, making it quite possible they also lied to the census taker. On a genealogy note, most residents were listed in census document in a very specific order, with the head of the household first, the spouse next, children in order of their birth, and then anyone else living there, such as servants, boarders, and in-laws, last. When the 1880 census was taken, Josephine's family was living with her half-sister Rebecca Weiner at 138 Perry Street. Henry and Sophie are listed in the correct order, but their children are in an odd order. Seventeen-year-old Henrietta was listed after Sophie as "without occupation," followed by twenty-three-year-old Nathan, who was a laborer, and then nineteen-year-old Josephine is listed next to last as "at home," just above a boarder. It's as if she and Nathan, who may not have been at home, were afterthoughts. These facts are hardly sufficient evidence to prove she was not in San Francisco when the census was taken, but they are a curious departure from normal census enumeration.

Sadie Mansfield arrived in Phoenix on February 13, 1880, from Gillette, which was also a stage stop to Tip Top for many years. That same week, John Behan registered at the Bank Exchange Hotel in

Josephine Sarah Marcus was Wyatt's last wife. This photo, believed to be of young Josephine, was taken in Prescott, Arizona Territory, in 1880, when she was twenty years old. COURTESY OF TOMBSTONE WESTERN HERITAGE MUSEUM

Phoenix. Two weeks later, on March 5, Prescott's *Weekly Journal Miner* announced Sadie had come up from Phoenix on March 2.

Johnny next ventured to the new silver mine town of Tombstone, where he became a deputy sheriff of the county in November 1880. About a month later, Josephine was also in the noisy mining community of Tombstone. She moved in with Johnny and his son, Albert, and by April 1881 she was signing letters as and calling herself Mrs. Josephine Behan. The *Tombstone Epitaph* reported on November 11, 1881, that an S. Mansfield had passed through Colton, California, bound for Arizona. It was around this time that Josephine came back from a trip only to find her dashing, womanizing husband in bed with another woman. Her biographer Mabel Cason recalled interviewing Josephine about Johnny's infidelity: "[She] told us about her time in Tombstone. . . . Finally, Johnny started running around with a married woman and neglecting her—and she met Wyatt Earp."[30] She left Behan and it's commonly believed she began to see Wyatt Earp around this time.

Like many other young, impulsive girls, Josephine wanted to be more than an average housewife. She loved life and sought opportunities to move up from the ranks of a poor Jewish girl, although not all of them worked out in her favor. She was a rebellious teenager who wanted a man to love her, and she wanted to live life on her own terms. She refused to live under the care and guidance of her obviously merciful, loving family. They were willing to take her back and hide her reckless past, and she seemed willing to return to them—but only until the urge for adventure hit again. She seemed to be constantly running to other things rather than away from her family.

She fell in love for the first time with the charming man-about-town, Johnny Behan, and he broke her heart. She then turned to Wyatt Earp, who was handsome, but quiet and stoic. With Johnny she had excitement, but with Wyatt she felt she had stability. Their romance blossomed, apparently secretly, in Tombstone. Even though Sadie traveled back to California in February 1882, she returned to Wyatt. The *Tombstone Weekly Epitaph* reported on February 27, 1882, that Mrs. S. Mansfield, of Tombstone, was among the eastbound passengers who had passed through Colton, California. Sadie Mansfield stayed in Tombstone while Wyatt was out on his Vendetta, and she appeared in Cochise County's 1882 census, which was taken in July. Josephine Marcus was not listed, but Johnny Behan and his son Albert were. All three were listed on different pages of the census.

In 1882 Josephine returned to San Francisco, where she met up with Wyatt Earp. According to a newspaper interview with Wyatt's brother Virgil, her future husband arrived in San Francisco in July 1882 and the July 9, 1882, *San Diego Union* reported, "*San Francisco Call*: Virgil Earp . . . has been in this city for several weeks past. . . . Virgil also states that his brother Wyatt will arrive in this city to-day [*sic*], and no warrant was ever issued for him or his brother." It's not known whether he actually arrived that day, as predicted.

The *Sacramento Daily Record-Union* reported on October 20, 1882, "Ex–United States Marshal Virgil Earp arrived in this city last evening from Tombstone, Arizona. He is here for the purpose of meeting his brother W.B. Earp, who will arrive from the east this morning." It seems odd the paper said Virgil was from Tombstone since he had moved to Colton in mid-September. It seems possible he and Wyatt returned to Tombstone in late 1882: The November 1, 1882, *Los Angeles Herald* reported both Wyatt and Virgil passed through Fresno on October 31, 1882, on a train that was headed either south or east.

In 1883 the *Sacramento Daily Record-Union* reported on April 6 that "the notorious Wyatt Earp" had passed through their town en route to Salt Lake City. The next day he checked into the Walker House in Salt Lake City, Utah, by himself. A month and a half later he had a letter awaiting him in Salt Lake City and in September, an S. Earp appeared on the ladies' unclaimed letter list. Lists for unclaimed letters, for both men and women, were posted in the local papers because of the transient lifestyle of the pioneers. Josephine and Wyatt then traveled to Galveston, Texas, where they checked in to the prestigious Washington Hotel on December 1, but were gone by December 23, 1883, when an unclaimed letter was listed for Mrs. Sadie Earp.[31] In March 1884 they returned to Salt Lake City, where they checked in to the Valley House Hotel. The local paper noted that Wyatt Earp and his wife of Dodge City, Kansas, had checked in. Later in 1884 Josephine and Wyatt had made their way to Eagle City, Idaho, near the soon-to-be mining boomtown of Coeur d'Alene, where he owned the White Elephant saloon. She and Wyatt shared the dream of striking it rich one day and they traveled to various mining towns in their quest. They made money on some of their mines, but in the end they were broke. They shared a love of racehorses, camping under the stars, and the adventure of finding the next big boom. At the end of September 1884 Wyatt and his wife and James and his wife checked into the St. Charles Hotel in Los Angeles. While no records have been found to prove that Josephine and Wyatt were legally married, they claimed they were married in 1885—at least that's what they told US census enumerator Ernest Grinton in 1910. It's also curious to note that Wyatt said he was married twice and Josephine just once. In her 1930 US census she stated she was first married at the age of forty, which would mean they were married in 1901.

Whether they ever really were married, Josephine and Wyatt were, in every appearance, husband and wife. In 1887 the couple headed to San Diego, where he invested in real estate. They not only bet on horses, but also owned their own and traveled the circuit. One of their horses, Atto Rex, proved a winner often, and took first in a trotting race in Sacramento on September 19, 1889. Sometimes when their horse won, Wyatt would buy Josephine jewelry. But jewelry wasn't the most important thing to her; she recalled, "Sometimes our fortunes were up, sometimes they were down, but there was always Wyatt with me and nothing mattered a great deal to me so long as I had him." She began to pawn her jewelry to her friend Lucky Baldwin to place her bets, and then she started to increase her bets, "with more fresh-handedness than wisdom." Despite Wyatt's displeasure, Josephine became addicted to gambling on the ponies, and Wyatt continued to buy back her jewelry. Fed up, Wyatt finally gave her an ultimatum: "You're not a smart gambler. And you have no business risking money that way. Now after this I'm not going to redeem any more of your jewelry." He also told Baldwin to stop loaning her money, but Josephine continued to gamble.[32]

They eventually moved to Yuma, Arizona, and took up mining, but when stories of Klondike gold began circulating, they ventured to the great Alaskan frontier. By 1898 they made their way to Rampart and settled into a small cabin where Josephine cooked and was part of the community. She fondly remembered that time: "As soon as we settled and I was taking my first batch of bread from the oven, with beans boiling on the stove, Wyatt came in from battling a snowstorm, dressed in his mukluks (boots) and parka. He sniffed, his eyes lighted up with pleasure, 'snug as a bug in a rug!' he exclaimed. On such small hinges does the door to contentment swing."[33] Two years later Josephine and Wyatt were in Nome, Alaska, where Wyatt had a saloon. Although Josephine generally stayed home, she did get involved in a community relief effort that summer to help recent victims of a violent ocean storm. While Wyatt was working at his saloon, Josephine found ways to keep herself occupied. Wyatt had told his friend Charlie Welsh that "Sadie," as he called her, gambled on their Alaska boat trips. She in turn said Wyatt had affairs with other women while in Alaska.[34] The ships that took passengers like Josephine and Wyatt were often quite luxurious. One such ship was called the *Queen* and operated during the Klondike gold rush. Edward Parkinson was a passenger and described what the ship looked like:

As soon as we were shown our state-rooms and had made ourselves at home with the surroundings, we commenced a tour of inspection of the floating palace that was to be our home for the next twelve days. Our rooms opened into the dining-room, in which there were three tables, one reaching the entire length of the room, and two shorter ones placed in the broadest part of the room. The social hall is on the main deck, and is reached by a flight of steps from the dining-room. It is well furnished with parlor furniture, including tables for games and an upright piano. At the stern of the vessel on the main deck is the smoking room, where games of chess and whist were played all day long excepting at meal times. In the bow and stern were convenient places for steamer chairs. The vessel was lighted with electricity, and every convenience was at hand.

In 1901 Josephine and Wyatt left Alaska for good and headed back to California—far better off than when they arrived. According to an interview Wyatt gave to the *Los Angeles Express* on December 12, 1901, "Wyatt Earp, the well-known sporting authority, passed the day in Los Angeles with his wife. He has just returned from Nome, where he has mining properties sufficient to make him financially comfortable for the rest of his life." While the money did last for a long time, it did not last the rest of their lives.

Josephine and Wyatt next traveled to the Nevada mines; in 1902 they settled in Tonopah, where Wyatt ran a saloon called The Northern. In 1905 Josephine and Wyatt met up with Virgil and his wife, Allie, in Goldfield, Nevada. Josephine and her husband lived there for a few years and then divided their time between their Happy Days mine in Vidal, California, and Los Angeles.

During this time Josephine became heavily involved in the editorial process of her husband's story, on which writer Stuart Lake was working. She did everything she could to make sure her husband's reputation was nothing less than stalwart. She also made sure her true story was never told. The following excerpt from one of Josephine's letters is just one example of how she fought for her man:

Dear Mr. Hart: I wish to thank you most sincerely in your very kind thoughts in contradicting the nasty and ugly articles which appeared in the Sunday Times *of March 12, 1922 regarding my husband. Mr. Earp only yesterday did learn of the unpleasant affair. I have called in the* Times *staff and have made it very plain to them that every untruth must be corrected and printed in the same sensational manner. I feel deeply indebted to you for your kindness to us. It was a mighty big thought of yours and we highly appreciate it. I am leaving for the mines today where my husband is at present and fully acquaint him of all this unpleasant affair and also tell him your genuine kindness to him. Accept our heartiest congratulations and wishing you and your wife every happiness in the world of which you are more than worthy. I wish to thank you once more for all you have done.*

Josephine was with her husband for forty-seven years, remaining at his side until he drew his last breath. Despite their differences, throughout their marriage Josephine and Wyatt shared a love of travel and betting on sporting events, crisscrossing the West in a number of adventures—all with hopes of striking it rich. Although their adventures ended with Wyatt's death from prostate cancer on January 13, 1929, in Los Angeles, Josephine continued to make sure her husband's reputation was never tarnished in the many stories written about him. She also forbid anyone from calling her Sadie and insisted she be called Josie.

Josephine Earp spent the rest of her days living in Los Angeles and visiting her sister in Oakland. When her sister died in 1936

Josephine Sarah Marcus was Wyatt Earp's last wife and spent forty-seven years with him. This photo was taken on July 4, 1921. Photos of young Josephine are as varied and as questionable as her past. This is one of the few verifiable photos of her.

Josephine fell into a depression. She eventually rebounded and found a new cause to keep her busy. She connected with Earp relatives Mabel Earp Cason and Vinnolia Earp Ackerman. She moved in with them and began telling her story. For four years they attempted to write it, but Josephine was evasive and slightly senile. That story was never published, but survives as the "Cason Manuscript."

She always made sure no one knew the true story of what happened while she was in Arizona, and in the end alienated close friends and family. Today her history is still somewhat of a mystery. Josephine Sarah Marcus Earp died of a heart attack on December 19, 1944, forever taking her secrets to the grave, just like she wanted.

CHAPTER TWO

Mr. & Mrs. Virgil Earp

"Even then when I was nine years old I was a mean-tempered, proud little cuss."

—ALLIE EARP

Virgil Walter Earp is probably the second best known of the Earp brothers and was made famous by Sam Elliott's portrayal in the 1993 movie *Tombstone*. He married his first wife at age seventeen and his last at age thirty. He was a farmer, served in the Civil War, and was a stage driver and lawman during his sixty-two years. Virgil was born to Nicholas Porter Earp and Virginia Cooksey Earp on July 18, 1843, in Hartford, Kentucky. He grew to be almost six feet tall, was of medium build, and sported chestnut hair, a sandy moustache, blue eyes, and a frank expression.

Virgil secretly married his first wife, Magdalena "Ellen" Rijsdam, in 1860, but because she was underage, her parents were against the marriage, as were his. Magdalena was born to Gerrit Rijsdam and Magdalena Catrina Van Velzen on November 25, 1842, in Utrecht, Netherlands. She arrived in the United States with her family on May 22, 1847, and her father worked as a peddler in Baltimore, Maryland. The Rijsdams soon made their way west, settling in Lake Prairie Township in Pella, Iowa, by 1850.

Since Ellen and Virgil both lived in Pella in July 1860 at their parents' respective homes, it's likely they met in town. No one knows why love connects two people, but it joined Ellen and Virgil's hearts together. Marriage records have not been found to verify whether they were ever married, and her family records indicate her father was not happy about the couple. Proof of their time together exists because Ellen and Virgil became the proud parents of Nellie Jane Earp—Virgil's only known child. She was born on January 7, 1862, and based on that, it's likely Virgil and Ellen were "together" around April 1861. Could it be that this seventeen-year-old woman, who was eight months older than Virgil, got pregnant without being married? If so, that might explain why her father was reportedly so upset. Only those who are no longer among us know the truth, and they're not talking.

Based on an 1889 newspaper story, the teenage lovers did not live together. It wasn't until Ellen's pregnancy began to show that they announced their marriage. When baby Nellie was about six months old her father enlisted in Company C of the 83rd Illinois Infantry Regiment on July 26, 1862, and left to serve in the Civil War. Later, having been told by her parents Virgil was killed in action, Ellen and Nellie moved to Oregon Territory with the Rijsdams as Virgil fought in the Civil War. There is no way she could have known he was still very much alive. Upon his return to Pella, Virgil discovered Ellen was gone, but whether he thought she abandoned him or died is unknown. He headed toward California and began a new chapter in his life without Ellen and Nellie.

Ellen, like Virgil, "married" three times. After Virgil, she married John Van Rossen on February 24, 1864. He died just two years later, in 1866. That same year, she married her last husband, Thomas Jackson Eaton, who passed away in 1891.[35] By that time, Virgil had already been married to his last wife, Alvira.

On April 21, 1899, Ellen and her daughter, Nellie, had a reunion with Virgil after thirty-nine years. The headline in the *Portland*

This rare photograph of Virgil Walter Earp at age nineteen was taken in 1862 in Monmouth, Illinois, by E. S. Cleveland. In California, Virgil was a saloon keeper in San Bernardino and a constable in Colton, and in 1887 became Colton's first city marshal. COURTESY OF NICK CATALDO

Oregonian on April 22, 1899, read, AFTER MANY YEARS, VIRGIL EARP MEETS HIS WIFE OF LONG AGO.

Were they star-crossed lovers like Romeo and Juliet? It seems likely, according to the account from the *Oregonian* (which erroneously noted Virgil as the older of the two):

> *Earp was married to his first wife, then Ellen Rysdam, at Oskaloosa, Ia., in February, 1860. He was then 17 years-old and she was still younger. The parents of both young people strenuously opposed the match—the girl's parents because they did not want their daughter, who was a native of Holland, to marry into an American family; Earp's because he was too young. So the wedding was kept secret, the couple got only an occasional opportunity to see each other, and not till the birth of their daughter did they make their union known. Then there was trouble on both sides of the house, which, however, was soon settled by the enlistment of Earp in the civil war.... His young wife was left with her parents, who continually urged her to secure a divorce from her husband, and who finally took it upon themselves to declare the union at an end. Soon word was received that Earp was wounded, then that he was dead, and his wife had no reason to doubt either report. With her parents she came west, bringing her child, and in 1867 she married Thomas Eaton at Walla Walla. In the meantime Earp returned to his home, found his wife gone, heard from friends that she had married again, and philosophically decided that the best thing he could do was to keep out of her way.*

The newspaper story also included some details about the nature of Virgil's visit:

> *All this time Mrs. Eaton was busy rearing a family of five children, the eldest of whom was Earp's daughter. . . . After a while*

she heard that there was nothing in the story about Earp's death, but under the circumstances she was not especially eager to renew the acquaintance. Even when she found that he had been keeping himself informed in a general way of her welfare and that of his daughter, there was no correspondence. Earp, having the second Mrs. Earp to care for, made no effort to restore the first wife to his fireside. Had circumstances been such that this was entirely agreeable, he was not at all sure that she still cared for him. The present reunion was brought about by the recent illness of Earp's daughter, Mrs. Law, who had learned the story of her father and discovered that his present residence was at Prescott, Ariz. She had been corresponding with him since September, and expected to make him a visit last winter, but a sudden attack of pneumonia changed her plans, and instead her father hastened to her bedside. He is now enjoying a very pleasant visit with her and his two grandchildren, at her home, which is near that of Mrs. Eaton, in North Portland. He will remain for several days more, before he starts on his journey home. Years have taken away the pain the meeting between the former husband and wife would once have caused and the little visit has been a most happy one for all.

Nellie recovered and lived thirty more years. She passed away on June 17, 1930, in Portland, Oregon.

Ellen died twenty years before Nellie, on May 3, 1910, in Cornelius, Oregon, and is buried in the Bertrand plot at River View Cemetery in Portland, where Virgil is also buried. According to the cemetery's website, "Virgil Earp is buried at River View Cemetery in Portland, Oregon because his daughter, Mrs. Janie [*sic*] Law lived in Portland at the time of his death."

After reading this newspaper account, knowing they're buried in the same cemetery plot, combined with the fact that Ellen's daughter

Anness Isabelle Eaton-Bertrand named her daughter Virgilene in 1900, lends to Ellen and Virgil's life being something akin to a Shakespearean tragedy.

In 1866 Virgil went to see his parents, who had moved to California. Shortly after that he ventured into the Southwest, where he spent a few years working various jobs.

By January 1870 he made his way back to the Midwest, settling in Peoria, Illinois. According to the 1870 *Peoria City Directory*, Virgil was working as a bartender on Irving Street in a saloon owned by William Vansteel, down the street from where a Peoria madam named Jane Haspel could be found. Since the young Earp brothers often traveled together, it's odd that Virgil went to Peoria alone before his brothers joined him. Just five short months later, Virgil married his second wife, Rozilla, and they were residing at his parents' home in Lamar, Missouri.

Very little is known of the second Mrs. Virgil Earp. In-depth research unearthed only three verifiable facts about Rozilla Draggoo. The first is that she was born around 1853 in France. The name Rosalie "Rosa" is French and is what appears on her census record, but was easily misspelled as Rozilla or Rosilla. The same is true for her last name, which according to a marriage record was spelled Draggoo. It could easily have been Dragoud, which is a French name, but was written as it sounded.

The second fact is that on May 28, 1870, a woman listed as Rozilla Draggoo legally married Virgil and the ceremony was performed by his father, Nicholas Porter Earp, who was justice of the peace at the time. The marriage was recorded on May 30, 1870. Marriage records during this time were merely pieces of paper written by the justice of the peace or minister. They were taken to the county recorder's office and filed or entered into a record book.

The last fact is that in September 1870 she and Virgil were living in Lamar, Missouri, with Virgil's parents. The newlyweds moved in with Virgil's parents, along with his sister Adelia and brother Warren. Nearby were half-brother Newton and his family, as well as Wyatt and his first wife, Aurilla.

Other records show that there was a Rauzilla Dragoo who would have been about the same age of Virgil's Rozilla, but further research and contact with her descendants have proved this cannot be the same woman. This Rauzilla was born in 1845 in Delaware County, Indiana, and married James R. Jones in 1864. She and Jones are in the 1880 census together in Indiana and it indicates they had children in 1867, 1869, and 1872. So unless she left her husband after the birth of her second child and returned to him before the birth of her third, she could not have been married to Virgil.

The 1870 census is the last known trace of Virgil's second wife. It is interesting to note that both Wyatt's first wife, Aurilla, and Rozilla were residing in Lamar at the same time—this is the last time either was heard from. It's been postulated that Aurilla died of typhus, which

This is the only known marriage record for Virgil Earp, even though he was married three times. Rozilla Draggoo was his second wife.
COURTESY OF BARTON COUNTY RECORDER OF DEEDS

leads one to wonder whether the same disease could have taken Rozil-la's life. Regardless, the most logical assumption to make from known records is that Virgil became a widower shortly after marrying Rozilla.

Between 1871 and 1872 Virgil met and married his third and last wife, Alvira "Allie" Packingham Sullivan. Allie may have been small in stature, but her feisty Irish personality made up for it. She was known to speak her mind, be as stubborn as a mule, and pull a flask from her boot.

Allie had a tragic childhood and attended school only until the first grade. She was born to a farm laborer, John Sullivan, and his wife, Louisa Jane Norman-Sullivan, in January 1851 in Florence, Nebraska. Her birth year varies from one census to another, but when the 1860 census was taken in July, her parents stated she was nine, thereby making her birth year 1851. Both her parents were born in Indiana and the couple was married in Platte County, Missouri, on October 4, 1842, by Revered James Baker of the Methodist Episcopal Church.

Allie's oldest sister, Melissa, was born in Missouri and by 1850 John and Louisa Jane, along with their daughters Melissa, Lydia, and Mary, moved to Fremont, Iowa. After 1857 the population of Florence declined steadily as Omaha became the dominant city in the area. By the time Allie was nine, the family had moved again, and were living about seven miles south of the recently formed and growing town of Omaha City, which is present-day Omaha. Allie recalled her mother's comments about her father: "I heard mother say he was a terrible restless man. Gettin' a piece of land and when it was all cleared off of trees and the brush burnt off and a nice cabin on it, move off and begin all over again." Allie claimed her odd middle name of Packingham came from a Missouri River steamboat that was named after a Civil War general. Her father used to sell the timber he was clearing to the ship and that's how she got her name. However, there are no records of any ship or Civil War general named Packingham. There is a General Edward Packenham, who was defeated and killed in New Orleans in a battle against Andrew Jackson during the War of 1812. That General Packenham served in the British army, but was an Irishman. Allie's father was Irish, so maybe he was familiar with the general and admired him. Also, Packenham was often misspelled in the papers as Packingham.

Despite her odd middle name, life for nine-year-old Allie was good. She and her siblings played in the nearby woods, watched Mormon carts pass by on their way to Utah, and often visited with the native peoples. Her father managed to support his ever-growing Irish clan, and her mother cared for her husband and children. Allie recalled to her biographer Frank Waters, "To see how pretty things were you wouldn't think it. The wild grapes and black haws, the hazelnuts, black walnuts, pink Sweet William and turkey peas. And the blackberries in the clearing and in the woods, wild plum trees just like tame ones. But we'd been here quite a spell, so Mother said, and father was getting restless. Like there was something about that sun settin' down across the prairie which just naturally kept drawin' men and wagons to it. We children wanted to go ourselves."

On March 16, 1861, Allie's father left to join the Civil War. He left behind his wife with eight children, including twin babies. Allie recalled, "Being so near the river and right on the path of the wagons, we got all kinds of news. Some of it, we children could see, kept making father nervous. One day I was standin' at the window of the cabin when a neighbor woman came in the door. 'Louise,' she said to my mother, 'this is an eventful day. You know the Duchess of Kent died.'" Allie recalled this moment because her mother's eyes were red from crying, but not over the death of the duchess. Allie recalled, "It was the day father went off to the Civil War." While Allie and her siblings may have been nervous about what came next, they could never have foreseen how quickly the life they had known would be forever changed.

About a year after John Sullivan left to join the cause, Allie's mother, Louisa, died of unknown causes. Allie recalled this tragic day: "The day she was to be buried I came in the cabin from the woods where I had been crying, and there in the empty room kneeling beside her coffin with their hands over their faces, were two blanket squaws. I always liked Indians since."

Allie and her siblings—sisters Melissa, Lydia, Mary, and Aldora, her younger brother Frank, and the twins—were split up. She remembered, "There were eight of us children left. . . . Nobody knew where father was, so every one of us was given to a different family. I hope they got better than me." Melissa was about nineteen and on her own, and Lydia and Mary were sixteen and fourteen, respectively. The twins—a boy named Calvin and a girl whose name is not known—were born sometime after July 1860 since they don't appear on the US census.

Because of her nature to speak her mind, Allie was shuffled from one foster home to the next. She never mentioned how long she spent at her foster homes, but it appears she lived in foster care from when her mother died until she was sixteen, when she moved in with her sister. Her first home was with the McGrath family, which consisted of two brothers who married two sisters. They were a southern family forced by the war from their home to Omaha. Allie hadn't been there long before deciding to run away. The culmination of several incidents led her to make that choice. First, "Grandmother" McGrath told Allie to give her granddaughter Betty a foot bath. Allie said, "If she'd said 'Allie, you go down and wash Betty's feet,' I'd have known what she meant. So I asked the cook what a foot bath was." The cook convinced little Allie that meant to put the girl's feet in ice-cold water, to which boiling water was added. Well, when innocent Allie tried this, Betty screamed and Grandmother McGrath chastised Allie. Grandmother said to her, "If you were a black girl down South I'd see you horsewhipped from top to bottom!" Allie advised her she wasn't black and she was not going to be horsewhipped!

Allie said life was never the same with the McGrath family after that, and while Betty and her grandmother enjoyed eating fresh brandied peaches for breakfast, Allie did not. When summer arrived the McGraths bought a barrel of peaches and stored them in the cellar. But before they were taken down, Grandmother found the scrawniest peach she could find and gave it to poor Allie. Once again Allie's old friend the cook told her she should go to the cellar every day and take one, which Allie did. No one would have suspected Allie, but one day Mrs. McGrath found a spice bag Allie used as a watch pocket in the peach barrel. A spice bag was typically made of cheesecloth and filled with various spices to cook with. Shortly after that, Allie was chatting with one of the Mrs. McGraths about heaven. She asked Mrs. McGrath if she thought her mother was in heaven. Mrs. McGrath replied that if Allie's mother was a good Christian, then yes, but if she wasn't, then no. Allie then replied, "Well, if my mother ain't up there, you won't ever get there!"

It was at that point that Allie decided to run away. When Mr. McGrath caught Allie trying to escape, he stopped her and told her to go back upstairs. Allie recalled liking him for making her stay—at least until Easter that following year. All the family went to the store to buy new clothes. Allie was told by Mrs. McGrath to inform Mr. McGrath to pick out a new pair of gaiters for Allie (gaiters were worn around the legs to protect boots or clothing). Mr. McGrath instead had Allie pick out a pair for herself, and then asked her if those were the ones she wanted. When she said yes, those were the ones she would like, he replied, "Well take them off and go home. You can't have them—you're going to run away." Allie recalled, "And for that I did. They never got me again."

She then found the family that had taken in one of her twin siblings, hoping they would take her as well. She played with little Calvin—"Cally," as she called him—by sticking her tongue out at him. Calvin's new mother slapped Allie and said, "Don't you dare touch him. I want him to get weaned away from the rest of you children." She refused to take Allie, but convinced the Thomas family to take her in. Allie never saw her brother again. Calvin later died of whooping cough. Allie never mentioned how old Calvin was when she visited him, nor did she mention knowing where Calvin's twin sister had been placed.

The Thomas family had a little girl named Tennessee and a three-year-old boy whom Allie was to care for. Allie didn't last long there after Mrs. Thomas whipped her with a willow stick for something she didn't do. She then was shuffled to the Portersfield family, who owned the Portersfield and Newton Dry Goods store. They had a little boy who died young, and when Allie told people around town about his death, the family wanted her gone.

Around 1867, when Allie was sixteen, she moved in with her sister Melissa, who had recently married and moved to the bustling town of Omaha. She stayed with Melissa for a while and then moved across the river to Council Bluffs, Iowa, and lived with a waitress. She recalled, "I never stayed in one place or in one family; I could wash dishes and scrub floors in one as well as another and they're both jobs I haven't seen no end to yet. Besides, I had a hankerin' to keep moving." Like her father, Allie had a wandering spirit, so it was fitting her future husband had the same zeal for travel.

Allie told her biographer she first met Virgil while she was waitressing at the Planters House on Dodge Street. Allie claimed the boardinghouse was in Council Bluffs, but there was no Planters House there, however, and there was one across the river in Omaha. She also mentioned her first paying job was in Omaha. If that was the case,

Alvira "Allie" Packingham Sullivan at age sixteen
GLENN BOYER COLLECTION, COURTESY OF SCOTT DYKE

then the couple had to have met before December 28, 1872, because the boardinghouse was out of business by then.[36]

Allie became a budding young woman who worked hard to make a life for herself—and not the old-fashioned way. She scrubbed floors, washed, and cleaned. While she was working at the boardinghouse, a tall, handsome stagecoach driver walked into her life. To her, it must have been like a dream come true. She recalled, "For there I was, waiting tables at the Planters House . . . when I first saw him. It was in the early evening before most of the customers came in, and I had just sat down with all the girls and some chambermaids to have our supper first. I don't know why I remember him comin' so plain. He was tall, just over six feet, blond, blue-eyed, and had a red moustache." She asked the other girls who he was and they said he drove a stage. She remembered the first time Virgil saw her, too. She said, "Virge saw me, too. He always said I was just getting ready to take a bite out of a pickle. . . . When I was mean he used to say I was just as sour. But mostly he said I was not much bigger than a pickle but a lot more sweet."

Allie wasn't necessarily taken with Virgil right away and thought she would "fancy" someone shorter, like herself, and dark. But nonetheless, she fell for the tall, handsome blond. According to Allie they were married about a year later in Council Bluffs. While no records have been found to prove their marriage, the 1900 US census lists them as being married in 1873, which would be about right.

About a year later, around 1874, Allie and Virgil, along with Virgil's brother Warren, parents Nicholas and Virginia, sister Adelia, and Adelia's future husband, Bill Edwards, headed to California. Adelia would become Allie's closest friend later in life. They stopped in Kansas to meet up with Virgil's older half-brother, Newton, and his family. The Earp party, as well as others, consisted of eleven wagons, with Nicholas acting as wagon master. The party then arrived in Dodge City, where they met Wyatt and Morgan. Allie told her biographer, "Only it wasn't happenstance that Morg and Wyatt were together—they had to be there." It's not clear just what Allie meant by that statement.

Deciding to wait until spring to continue on to California, and feeling Dodge City was too rough, nine of the eleven wagons in the Earp caravan headed north and settled in Peace, Kansas, which was near Sterling, while Allie's husband, Virgil, and his brother Wyatt stayed behind. Virgil told Allie he was staying because Wyatt, as city marshal of Dodge, needed his help. Morgan also stayed for a while, but then headed to Butte, Montana.

Allie recalled living in Peace, "a sleepy little Quaker town where all the other wagons were waiting. There we rented a house. The whole family with nothing else to do got religious and went to church practically all winter. One Sunday Grandma Earp, as they all called Virginia, heard a sermon about a baby dying before it was baptized and was therefore condemned to roast in hell." Apparently it was the last time Grandma Earp ever set foot in a church. Allie said, "After that, she sat at home and smoked her old pipe in peace—in Peace all right!"

On May 8, 1877, they packed up their wagons and got back on the trail as the prairie flowers were starting to blossom. Virgil was back with the family and they once again had eleven wagons going to California. After crossing the plains and camping at various places along the way, they stopped in a small valley just two days out from Prescott, Arizona. When Allie and Virgil went up to speak with the owners of a nearby log house, they learned it was a small post set up to handle the mail from Prescott. It was owned by Mr. Jackson and his brother-in-law, Ben Baker. The Jacksons already had four children, and Judy Jackson was ready to give birth to number five.

The Jacksons asked Allie to stay on and cook and help Judy with the children. Virgil was offered wages if he would make the two-day ride to Prescott each week. Allie and Virgil talked about the offer. They were planning to stay in Prescott anyway and they had only one silver

half-dollar to their name. Knowing they needed money to start their
new life in Prescott, they accepted the Jacksons' offer. Allie said, "Well,
it seems that this is as good a place as any for a start." Virgil replied, "I
reckon." They emptied out their belongings from the wagon, and said
their good-byes, and the rest of the family headed on to California. Virgil worked the mail route and Allie cooked and cared for the Jackson
family. After Judy Jackson gave birth to Jimmy, the Jacksons decided to
head back to Missouri. By October 1877 Allie and Virgil were living
in Prescott, which had just become the capital again for the territory of
Arizona. It was a bustling town with saloons, dry-goods stores, and restaurants that served as a supply base for miners and prospectors. When
Allie and Virgil arrived, eggs were selling for 75 cents per dozen (about
$16 today) and calico for making clothes was 25 cents per yard.

Virgil's half-brother Newton and his wife, Jennie, were already in
Prescott and had taken up residence in an old house next to a deserted
sawmill. It wasn't anything special, but it did have bathtubs and wall-
paper. Allie and Virgil moved in with them and Virgil continued driving the mail route, while Allie was in charge of making the daily bread.
When Newton and Jennie headed back to Kansas about six weeks
later, Allie and Virgil took over their house. Virgil quit his mail route,
filed a timber claim, and cleared the land, where he built a log cabin
into which he and Allie eventually moved. He also did a little pros-
pecting and while he was away Allie ventured around Prescott.

She and Virgil became friends with Sheriff James Dodson, who
was considered one of the toughest lawmen of his day. According to
genealogical records, his great-grandfather was Daniel Boone. Around
October 1877 Dodson deputized Virgil. Allie, like other pioneer
women of the day, grew lonely and rarely saw anyone at her cabin, save
for a lonely prospector here and there. One day, an Indian boy who had
adopted a hunting dog he found in the woods walked up to the cabin.
The dog went in the cabin, smelled around and jumped in Allie's bed.

Virgil Walter Earp posed for this photograph in the 1880s. Despite losing the use of his left arm in an assassination attempt, Virgil returned to law enforcement. COURTESY OF ROBERT G. MCCUBBIN

The Indian boy said to Allie, "Him like bed. Me sleep under tree. Him white-man dog. You keep." And with that, Allie had a companion. She named the dog Frank, after her brother.

Allie never lost her girlish spunk or sass, and even Virgil was the recipient of it occasionally. She recalled a time when an old prospector stopped by and criticized Virgil, who was away, for making his wife chop wood. The Dutchman said to Allie, "Damn a man who won't chop wood for his wife," to which Allie replied, "I say damn a man who won't provide any wood for his wife to chop!" Even though Allie had defended Virgil, she had plenty of time alone to think about what the old prospector had said. So one day when she and Virgil were build-ing a corral together, she struggled to carry the heavy logs. She felt compelled to help because she knew Virgil couldn't build it alone. But when the weight became too much, she said, "I can't hold this much longer, Virge." He replied back, "Oh yes you can. Be a big man now." Virgil finally came to her rescue and placed the log over his broad shoulder, but it slipped. Allie said to him, "Now lift it up yourself; I ain't no man," and stormed off into the house.

They spent about two years in Prescott and had a comfortable lit-tle cabin, a well-stocked corral, a profitable timber claim, a Studebaker wagon, and horses. Nevertheless, both Allie and Virgil were either cursed or blessed with a wandering spirit. That spirit was renewed when news of Ed Schieffelin's silver discovery, in a little town called Tombstone, made its way to Prescott. Virgil sent letters to Wyatt and James in Dodge and to Morgan, who was in Montana. Allie remembered the fall day in 1879 when Virgil's brothers arrived in Prescott. Virgil came running into the clearing to see Wyatt and his wife, Mattie, and James and his wife, Bessie, along with her teenage daughter, Hattie. They were told that Morgan and his wife were coming in from Butte, Montana Territory.

Since space in the wagons was limited, the brothers and sisters-in-law spent two days planning and discussing what could be taken and what had to stay behind. From horse tack to basic household items, there had to be sacrifices—even Allie and Bessie's rolling pins were laid side-by-side so the best one could be selected. Even though Allie's was made of fine-grained hardwood, and made by hand from a neighbor, it wasn't as symmetrical as Bessie's, so Allie's was left behind. Bessie had a large commode and Allie remembered it taking up a lot of space and "not bein' any good." Allie's prize possession was a sewing machine Virgil had given her and the first one she ever owned. It was so big that Virgil told her she had to leave it behind. Allie being Allie said, "All right, Virge. Leave it behind. I'll stay with it." She recalled there being a long silence at that moment until Wyatt broke it. He came over and said, "Oh, we can get it in someplace." Allie also recalled him saying under his breath, "but I don't know where." Just before Virgil headed for Tombstone, US Marshal Crawley Drake appointed him as a US deputy marshal.

It turns out Allie's fight for her sewing machine was beneficial. When they got to Tombstone, the town's population was exploding. In June 1880 the population was about 2,000, which was a little more than double that of the previous year. Such items as water, food, and cloth were expensive. Allie recalled, "Everything was nice if you had money, but we didn't so it wasn't." Allie, along with Wyatt's wife, Mattie, put Allie's sewing machine and their skills to good use. Since Allie was one of a handful of people in town who had a machine, she began sewing for people in Tombstone. They charged one cent per yard and even made a large tent from a canvas for one of the new saloons. Allie said, "With double rows of stitching on that we like to got rich."

While Allie and Virgil never got rich in Tombstone, they did manage to earn some money. They attended an occasional play at Schieffelin Hall, but mostly the women stayed home—with the exception of the day she and Wyatt's wife, Mattie, ventured into town alone and returned home drunk. Allie said all they wanted to do was see the fancy hotels and restaurants in town. She recalled, "Everything would have been jim-dandy, but Wyatt and Virge came home for dinner for the first time during that hot spell." (Dinner during that time meant the afternoon meal.)

Proper breakfast, lunch, and dinner etiquette had its place in the 1880s and breakfast was considered the least formal of the meals. It's doubtful that Allie and the other Earp wives followed proper etiquette to the letter, but it's likely they abided by some of the rules. Generally the table was set simply with a tablecloth (if available), napkins, plain white china or dishes, a kettle for coffee, a pat of butter in crystal, and glasses. The table center would have held flowers or fresh fruit, and a loaf of bread with a large slicing knife was also on the table. In addition to bread, breakfast may have included such items as hominy or buck-wheat, with molasses or butter. Milk was also a staple at the breakfast table. In colder weather, bacon, sausage, whitefish, sliced cold meat, and hot steak or chops were served. Cold meats or meat pies, because of their hacked joints or rugged pastry, were placed on a sideboard because they did not "look good" with the other delicate items on the table. Fresh fruit and eggs were always a welcome breakfast treat. This was the meal where the Victorians "let their hair down" and relaxed. Even their attire was less formal, with a woman wearing an early morning inside dress, which was not acceptable in most other situations.

Allie recalled the Earp wives had nice dresses, but rarely got to wear them, "and we never had a bunch of friends. . . . The line was pretty well drawn those days. Ordinary women didn't mix with the wives of gamblers and saloon keepers and bartenders no matter what pretty dresses they had or how nice they were. And the Mrs. Earps were all good, but they were in that fix and we just naturally didn't have much to do with them." Being a gambler was a respectable occupation in the Victorian West, but being a wife of a gambler was not.

For reasons unknown, Allie boarded a stagecoach on August 4, 1880, and went to the Earp family home in San Bernardino. The

Epitaph reported, "Mrs. Virgil Earp departed yesterday's stage for a visit to her old family home in San Bernardino. We wish her a pleasant trip and speedy return." While there she would have visited with Virgil's parents and Morgan's wife, Louisa, who was living there at the time. It's odd her sister-in-law Louisa never mentioned meeting Allie in her letters to her sisters during this time.

Given Allie's independent mind and often cantankerous attitude, one has to wonder if she abided by proper stagecoach etiquette of the day. When riding in a carriage, coach, or buckboard, certain rules applied to female passengers. If the passengers consisted of one man and one woman and they rode in a two-seated carriage, the lady was always given the seat on the right, facing the horse or horses. A lady always entered the carriage with her back to the seat so she did not have to turn around in the carriage. A gentleman was also required to be careful not to tread on a woman's dress. A lady never descended from a carriage before a man, even if the man had to climb over her to get out.

A lady also was expected to trust her driver and not interfere with their driving, unless she feared for her life. If that happened, she was allowed to "delicately" suggest a change, and then apologize for making the suggestion. It was considered very offensive if a lady did interfere. She was supposed to sit quietly and calmly during the course of a drive. That hardly sounds like Allie.

Allie returned to Tombstone, although when is unknown, and lived in her little adobe home. Life was quiet for her and her sisters-in-law, until October 1881 when the gunfight took place behind the OK Corral. Allie and the other Earp wives were in their homes. Mattie was putting her hair up in curlers and Allie and Louisa were sewing two rugs together. Allie told her biographer Frank Waters, "Lou and me were sewin' that carpet together when all of a sudden guns started poppin'. We stopped. The noise was awful it was so close—just a couple short blocks up the street. Lou laid down her hands in her lap and bent her head. I jumped up and ran out the door. Nothin' could ever keep me from Virge when I thought he was in danger. Mattie was outdoors. Her hair was done up in curlers and she was ashamed to have people see them so she ran back inside the house." On her way toward the gun-fight, the butcher's wife, whom Allie passed, slapped a floppy sunbon-net on Allie's head. Allie said, "They had carried Virge to a drug store. He was lyin' just outside. When I got up to him a big man pushed aside the crowd and hollered, 'Stand back boys; let his old mother get in!' He meant me! And I was eleven years younger than Virge. It was that sun-bonnet I guess." She remembered kneeling down beside her husband as the doctor was probing around for the bullet. He never found it and finally gave up. Turns out the bullet passed clean through his calf. He was then carried back to their house. Both Virgil and Morgan recov-ered from their injuries and Allie believed all was well.

She remembered the night of December 28, 1881, when her beloved Virgil was shot again. She said, "We'd had a right good Christ-mas dinner. We still had some nuts left over and some of the pepper-mint candy Virge liked. We were sittin' up, waitin' for him to come home and eat them . . . me and Lou [Louisa] believed all the trouble had blown over. About eleven-thirty we heard a sudden roar, loud, but far off. Fifteen minutes later—just before midnight, there was a knock on the door. I didn't have to open it. I knew what kind of news was there waitin'. I got my hat and coat and went runnin' out the door."

Resident and diarist George Parsons recalled that terrible night: "Tonight about 11:30 Doc. G. [Goodfellow] had just left . . . when four shots were fired in quick succession from very heavily charged guns, making a terrible noise and I thought were fired under my window, under which I quickly dropped. I immediately thought Doc had been shot and fired in return, remembering the latest episode and know-ing how pronounced he was on the Earp-Cowboy question. He had crossed though and passed Virgil Earp, who crossed to West side of 5th and was fired upon when in range of my window by men, two or three, concealed in the timbers of the new 2-story adobe going up for the Huachuca Water Co. He did not fall, but re-crossed to the Oriental and was taken from there to the Cosmopolitan, being hit with buckshot and badly wounded in the left arm with flesh wounds above the thigh."

Doctor Goodfellow had asked Parsons to get him some supplies and returned to Allie and Virgil's room at the hotel. He wrote, "Hotel well guarded, so much so that I had a hard trouble to get to Earp's room. He [Virgil] was easy. Told him I was sorry for him. "It's Hell, isn't it!" he said. His wife was troubled. "Never mind, I've got one arm left to hug you with," he said.

Allie told her biographer, "Men from the saloon came runnin' and carried him to the hotel and put him on a table. When they took off his shirt I almost cried." She watched as Dr. Goodfellow removed the rest of Virgil's shirt and nearly fainted. She recalled, "A load of buckshot had hit him in the side and back . . . and then I saw his left arm. It was the worst. A load of slugs had hit him in the elbow. It was awful lookin'." Virgil did not want to lose his arm, so he made Wyatt promise he wouldn't let Dr. Goodfellow remove it. Instead, the doctor removed several inches of bone. It was after this attempt on his life that the entire Earp family moved into the Cosmopolitan Hotel on Allen Street. Virgil eventually recovered but lost the use of his arm.

About three months later, Morgan Earp was assassinated while playing pool at Campbell & Hatch's Saloon. Within two days of his murder, Virgil and Allie left Tombstone for good and were headed to Colton, California, to be with family and bury Morgan. Allie recalled, "We got to Colton and Virge had to carry his arm in a sling for over two years. He finally got well in his back, but was always disabled in his left arm."

Although the majority of firsthand accounts of Virgil's life were recounted by Allie to her biographer, Virgil gave an interview to the

San Francisco Examiner in May 1882, in which he recalled the general atmosphere of Tombstone:

> *I was born in Kentucky but was raised in Illinois and Iowa. My parents came to this state, settling in San Bernardino, near Colton, at which later place they now live. I served for a little over three years in the war, in an Illinois regiment, and then came to California in 1866. I soon went into New Mexico, Arizona and all that southern country, where I have spent nearly six years. When Tombstone was discovered I was in Prescott. The first stage that went out of Prescott toward Tombstone was robbed. Robberies were frequent and became expensive, and the disordered condition of the new country soon brought a demand for the better protection of business and money, as well as life. I was asked to go to Tombstone in my capacity as United States Marshal, and went. My brother Wyatt and myself were fairly well treated for a time, but when the desperate characters who were congregated there, and who had been unaccustomed to troublesome molestation by the authorities, learnt that we meant business and determined to stop their rascality, if possible, they began to make it warm for us. The Tombstone country is of a peculiar character, the community being unsettled and dangerous. Most of the business men there stayed simply to make money enough to live somewhere else comfortably, and of course the greatest object with them is to have as much money as possible spent in the town and to get as much of it as they can, careless of the means of dispensation or the results of rough manners. Aside from the legitimate business men the bulk of the residents are idle or desperate characters, most of them coming into town broke and depending upon the gambling tables or criminal ventures to supply them with means of livelihood and dissipation."* [37]

In 1886, Virgil opened a detective agency in Colton. True to Allie and Virgil's wandering spirit, they traversed the West. About every two to three years found Allie and her husband on a new adventure. She recalled, "We were in Vanderbilt for three years and were livin' in Goldfield when Wyatt came through, and a dozen other towns and camps in Nevada and California during those twenty years. All those mining camps out on the desert were just alike, rows of adobes or old shacks or tents with wooden floors, and things so rough all the women had to walk down the middle of the road. Why, I got in the habit so of doin' that, that in San Bernardino I started walkin' down the middle of the street when it was a big town and blame near got run over."

Even though Allie wasn't Virgil's first true love, they shared a special bond. She doted on him and he adored her. In 1888, when he made out his will, he acknowledged just how he felt about his spunky, outspoken wife. He stated, "I, Virgil W. Earp, of the City of Colton, County of San Bernardino, and State of California, for and in consideration of the love and affection which I bear towards my wife, and as an expression of my heartfelt gratitude to her for constant, patient and heroic attendance of my bedside while I lay dangerously wounded at Tombstone, Arizona, do grant unto my wife, Mrs. Alvira Earp, as her separate estate, all that real property situated in the City of Colton, County of San Bernardino, State of California."

Although Allie and Virgil never had children, she couldn't have been happier when Virgil and his daughter, Nellie Jane, were reunited. She recalled, "There! All these twenty or more years and we'd never had a baby, and here was Virge findin' out for the first time in his life he had a grown-up young lady daughter named Jane!" Either Virgil knew about Nellie Jane like the 1899 *Oregonian* newspaper stated and never told Allie, or the reporter had been mistaken on that account.

Six years later, on October 19, 1905, Virgil died of pneumonia at the age of sixty-two. At the time Allie and Virgil were living in the mining town of Goldfield, Nevada, still chasing their dreams and appeasing their restless spirits. His daughter, Nellie Jane, had requested he be buried with her, along with his first wife, Magdalena, in Portland, Oregon, and Allie graciously obliged. Their life together in Tombstone and all over the West had brought Virgil and Allie Earp adventure and tragedy. Despite it all, Allie remained a feisty, funny, and caring woman who faced her challenges on the frontier head-on. She suggested to her biographer Frank Waters that her epitaph should read, "Here lies the body of Alvira Packingham. She's dead as hell and she don't give a damn!" Allie never did get that tombstone inscription and she passed away on November 11, 1947, in Los Angeles at the age of ninety-six. She's interred with her sister-in-law Adelia Earp Edwards, who was the only living sister of the Earp brothers.

This photograph of Alvira Packingham Sullivan was taken circa 1881. She was Virgil's last wife and his partner until he died.
COURTESY OF TOMBSTONE WESTERN HERITAGE MUSEUM

CHAPTER THREE

Mr. & Mrs. Morgan Earp

"There's not a joy this world can give like it takes it away. When the glow of early thoughts decline in feelings dwell decay. 'Tis not on youths smooth cheek the blush alone which fades so fast. But the tender bloom of heart is gone ere youth itself is past."
—LOUISA A. HOUSTON-EARP, 1880

Morgan was the youngest of the Earp brothers involved in the street fight behind the OK Corral. He was born Morgan Seth Earp on April 24, 1851, in Iowa and by the time he was nine years old, the Earp family was living in Pella, Iowa. While their older brothers worked on the farm with their father, Morgan and Wyatt attended school and their younger siblings, Warren and Virginia, stayed home with their mother. The family moved between Iowa, Kansas, Missouri, Illinois, and California until Morgan's parents settled in California in the 1860s.

Virgil's wife, Allie, remembered Morgan as "the nicest to us of all the Earps, the most good-natured and handsomest . . . his face wasn't lean like Jim and Wyatt's or heavy like Virge's, but more sensitive. His thick straight hair never did stay combed and his moustache was always scraggly."

According to researcher Kenneth Vail, "He was in no hurry to join his brothers in Tombstone and was doing quite well for himself in Montana." Morgan followed his brothers around the West, but no

Morgan Seth Earp married just once and was killed in Tombstone, Arizona, at the young age of thirty while playing a game of pool.
COURTESY OF ROBERT G. MCCUBBIN

definitive records could be found for Morgan Seth Earp in 1870. However, his brother James C. Earp was residing at Deer Lodge in Montana Territory that year. Just a few names down the list from James is a man named Seth Morgan, whose age is the same as Morgan's. Their rooms were right next to each other and Morgan and his roommate were both at work, which would have restricted census enumerator Wesley Jones from gathering the exact details. However, the place of birth states Tennessee, so the Morgan in this record may or may not be Morgan Earp. Deer Lodge was founded in the 1850s by John Grant when he established what would become one of the largest ranching operations in the country, which is still in operation today. In early 1870s, Deer Lodge was selected as the site for the Montana Territorial Prison, which was built by convict labor, and opened in 1871.

Morgan eventually made his way to Missouri, and a January 1875 St. Louis, Missouri, business directory lists Morgan as a bartender living at 424 S. Third Street. By September he had joined his brothers in Wichita, Kansas, and was fined for being arrested during a raid on a brothel run by a woman named Ida May. Since his brother Wyatt was on the police force, Morgan never paid the whopping $3 fine. According to researcher Kenneth Vail, "Ida May threw a party for seven couples. Ironically Morgan's girl Nellie Spalding never paid her fine either—thanks to Wyatt." By June 1876 Morgan, along with his older brother Wyatt, had made his way to the rough and rowdy cowtown of Dodge City, Kansas.

After that he made his way back to Montana, first to Miles City in October 1877, and according to the Butte–Silver Bow Public Archives, Morgan was in Butte by late 1879. It was likely in Montana or possibly Kansas that Morgan met his wife, Louisa Alice Houston. Louisa was the daughter of H. Samuel Houston and Elizabeth Waughtal and was born January 24, 1855, in Wisconsin. She was the second eldest of twelve children.[38] Today her great-nephew pronounces her name "Lou-I-sa." She was petite, loved flowers, wrote poetry, and kept a positive attitude despite living with a debilitating illness for most of her adult life. She suffered from rheumatoid arthritis and eventually "dropsy," which is now called edema and is the buildup of fluid in the body.

Her father was a farmer and the Houston family lived in Arena, Wisconsin, until 1870, when Louisa was fifteen. Arena was a railroad town where local farmers from Barneveld and Ridgeway drove their herds to the stockyards. Rumors have circulated that Louisa was the daughter of General Sam Houston, but that can't be true. Old Sam would have been sixty-two when she was born and it appears he was never in Wisconsin. Another story says her father was an illegitimate son of the general, but again, there is nothing to substantiate this.

Just when Louisa left Wisconsin is unknown. Family rumors have been passed down that she and her younger sister Kate left at an early age to become Harvey Girls, serving as waitresses in Harvey House restaurants at railroad stops. However, that theory is unlikely because Fred Harvey didn't implement his server standards until the 1880s. In a move to establish a reputation of exemplary service for Harvey House restaurants, in 1883 Fred Harvey began hiring his white-only female serving staff. The Harvey Girls, as they were known, needed to be single, educated, and well-mannered Americans. He placed ads in local newspapers that read, "White, young women, 18 to 30 years of age, of good character, attractive and intelligent." Their uniform consisted of a starched black and white ensemble with a skirt that hung no more than eight inches off the floor, opaque black stockings, and black shoes. Even though there was limited service in Kansas (and before the women were even called Harvey Girls) a little earlier than 1883, Louisa was living in California with Morgan's parents in 1880.

Sometime after the 1870 census was taken on July 27, Louisa had left home. Based on her own letters, around 1872 she was in Mason

This photo of Louisa Houston, Morgan Earp's wife, has never been published before. COURTESY OF LYMAN HANLEY

City, Iowa, where she posed for a portrait. She wrote to her sister Agnes, "Have you got one of my pictures I had taken in Mason City? The first one I ever had taken." She later wrote in 1882, "I believe Uncle Bill has one of my pictures I had taken in Mason City. Please tell him if he will send it to me to have one struck off it, I will return it to him with many thanks. It has been taken about ten years ago." She also wrote to Agnes in that same letter, "Do you remember the wild honeysuckle you pressed and sent to me more than seven years ago?" By this letter, one can surmise that in 1875 she obviously had not been living near her sister.

No records exist as to how, when, or where Louisa met Morgan. What is known is that Morgan traveled from St. Louis, Missouri, in 1875 to Wichita, and then to Dodge City, Kansas, by June 1876. He was also in Deadwood, South Dakota, and left that wild mining town in September 1877 on a pack train and arrived in Miles City, Montana, the following month. The pack train consisted of twenty-five people, including William and Frank Reece, Ranger Hank Wormwood, a man named Fitzsimmons, John McCormick, a few of their ladies, and two other men. It's possible Louisa was in this group.

While it cannot be determined where Morgan and Louisa met, they were in Montana together. A clue comes from some individual portraits taken in Butte, Montana. Louisa's was done by photographer A. J. Dusseau, who was first in Deer Lodge in 1874 and then in 1877 moved to Butte, where he became a well-known photographer until his death in 1908. While at Dusseau's, Louisa may have discovered some relief from her illness at the nearby Pipestone Hot Springs in Butte. Every Tuesday a coach picked up rheumatoid visitors like Louisa near Dusseau's studio and took them to Pipestone. Louisa and Morgan traveled from Butte to Miles City, Montana, between 1877 and 1879. According to researcher Kenneth Vail, "In Miles City (1877) they had a nice log cabin with plenty of space on the edge of town. Then they sold it in April 1878 and moved to a homestead ranch out on the

This photo of Louisa Houston was taken in Butte, Montana, by A. J. Dusseau, Photographic Art Gallery. COURTESY OF LYMAN HANLEY

Tongue River, no more than three miles from town." Nothing could be found to determine where or when they were married, but Morgan's sister, Adelia, said it was Prescott, Arizona.

Louisa and Morgan called Miles City, Montana, home for a couple of years. In 1879 a man named F. M. Wilson wrote a detailed description of this growing town:

On the south bank of the Tongue River, surrounded by a grove of magnificent cottonwoods stands the town of Miles City. We had expected to find a place such as Bismarck was in 1873, a collection of log and canvas buildings with a preponderance of saloons, gambling and dance halls, but in this we were disappointed. The town is built on two sides of a square [now Riverside Park] and the buildings are principally substantial frame structures, neatly painted and well kept. Some are of hewn logs, but the canvas element is entirely lacking. We were fairly surprised at the amount of business done, the large and complete stocks of goods kept by the merchants and the population of the place. Already the town has 700 inhabitants, a population nearly as large as Bozeman. The heaviest line of goods is kept by Broadwater, Hubbel and Company, who have a fine two story building and a large warehouse, in both of which every inch of spare room is closely packed with merchandise. . . . Paul McCormick & Company also have a fine two story building, neatly painted. Their store contains a little of everything, from confectionery to bed quilts, and in the labyrinth of supplies which crowd the shelves and counters, we notice clotheslines, neckties, watered ribbons and fine robes. Savage and Ninninger have a varied assortment of goods beginning with groceries and running up through clothing, fire arms and ammunition, terminating finally in spiritual things in the shape of liquid comforts for the inner man. . . .

But with a great deal that is good, there is still much that is evil in this young city. One evening, we were attracted by the music of a violin and piano to a building which we found to be a dance hall and in full blast. The air was lively, and the dancers evidently bent on having a good time. The men, judging from the fringed buckskin jackets, army blue and California overalls, belonged to a class of hunters and "bull-whackers," which is a large element here, while the blue is supplied by the garrison at Fort Keogh. The ladies, perhaps, were good, but not beautiful. One fair one we observed had a black eye and another appeared to have been recently at war. We did not take part in that dance. Things seemed a little too uncertain. We were not ambitious of sticking plaster, and so far as our teeth are concerned, we didn't want to part with any of them for, as an article of diet, they are not desirable. There are many faro banks in operation, and the click of the chips is constant day and night. One of the popular saloons is kept by William Reece, who makes a specialty of fine quality champagne, wines and liquors. A Steinway piano, under the skillful fingers of an excellent musician, is a great attraction, while papers of many kinds help to pass the tedious hours away. Chris Hehli, the tonsorial artist of the place, will shave a man, or scalp him, as the case requires, guarantees a neat job, and charges a reasonable price. . . . The number of boats arriving from Bismarck and other points on the river below during the season was 54. The first to arrive was the General Sherman, *and the last was the* F. Y. Batchelor. *For a large part of the trade, the town depends on the garrison at Fort Keogh. Some idea of the large amount of money disbursed at this post may be had from the fact that this season the government purchased 3,200 tons of oats and corn, 5,800 tons of hay and 7,500 cords of wood. The grain was brought from the east, but the coming season a large portion of it will be raised in the valley.*

According to researcher Kenneth Vail, "From Miles City, Morg escorted Lou to the Union Pacific rail-head for her first visit back home to Mason City. He went on to Butte where she joined him later. Morg entrusted her with the money management. When he had to return to Butte for the policeman job on September 1, 1879, she had to stay behind to close the deal at Miles City to sell their homestead property. Then, after the September 6 transaction was recorded, I have to assume that Lou then put the $1,000 in her purse on the coach for five days (layover at Bozeman) to Butte. That's some pretty rough traveling."

The following excerpt was found in the Butte City Council records: "On December 16, 1879 . . . moved, seconded, and carried that Daniel Brownwell, Morgan Earp, and Daniel Meikeljohn be and is hereby appointed Policeman for the City of Butte and that certificates of this appointment, under the seal of this city, be issued to them by the clerk." But Morgan's career as a Butte policeman was short-lived. By February 1880, he and Louisa had departed Butte for good, making half of the coach trip to Idaho on regular wheels, and the second half on sleighs. According to Vail, "It was absolutely spectacular beauty going up over Monida Pass and down to the RR terminus at Beaverhead, now Pocatello, Idaho and then they took a train for a few days en route to San Bernardino."

In March 1880 Morgan and his wife arrived at his parents' house in Temescal, California. The couple stayed with his parents for awhile, but since Louisa was sickly, Morgan left her at his parents' house and she joined him in Tombstone later.

Louisa penned this letter to her sister Agnes once she arrived at her in-laws' home in Temescal:

Temescal, California
March the 5th, 1880
   Dear Sister Agnes.[39] *I again take my pen in hand to let you [know this] evening and on Thursday we came by team to the*

Temescal Mountains Warm Springs. It is a very pretty place to live, and I suppose I will have to live here now for some time for there is no way to make money to get away. I am so far from the United States now that I feel as though I shall never get back again. They are all very old fashioned people,[40] *and I like it very much. They have a nice bath house where the warm water runs out of the mountains and an orchard of lemons and oranges. The trees are full of lemons, but the peach trees are in bloom, and everything is green, and there is so many wild flowers. I have been out gathering some to press. It is wonderful for the people to come to the springs that are sick. There are fourteen rooms, but there is no sick people here now because they say it is too cold weather. The people in this country don't know what cold weather is. They say it snowed two inches here this winter. The people that lived here for twenty years never saw any snow before. It is thirty miles to San Bernardino. I have got a chance to send my letter to town so I must close. Give my love to all my people and tell Bashford*[41] *to write. Give this money to mother. So good by,*

From your sister, Louisa Houston to Agnes Houston

Her next letter to Agnes was two months later:

Temescal, San Bernardino Co.
California
May the 3rd, 1880

Dear Sister Agnes,

I received your most kind and wonderful letter several days ago, and after several unsuccessful attempts to answer, I at last seat myself to write a few lines hoping those few lines will find you all well and happy as they now have me for I think the climate of

California is improving my health very much. I have received one letter from Bashford since I have been here and answered it. I got Olive's[42] letter the same day I got yours. I have also answered it and sent her a lot of pressed flowers. I put them in a magazine and sent them. I guess they will go all right. We have not many tame flowers on the place, but the hills and valleys are covered with all kinds. I have planted some and they are coming up nice. When they blossom, tell Olive I will press some and send to her, but of course it will be a long time yet. I have not went visiting to any of the neighbors yet, but I heard they have nice flowers, and I am going to try to get some to press if I can. Do you remember the wild honeysuckle you pressed and sent to me more than seven years ago? I have got it yet, just as nice as it ever was. I want you to gather the first wild flower you see blossoming and press it for me. I have almost lost hopes of getting that picture, but of course it will be better late than never. Well I can't think of anything to write that will interest you.

I think Bessie[43] is very pretty, and mother[44] looks so natural all except the ruffle on her neck for I never saw her wear one before, and it don't look right. Can't you get one of papa's pictures? I would like to have one so much. When I get some money I am going to send it and get all my brothers pictures.

You did not tell me if you got a letter on the fifth of March from me. I sent twenty dollars in it for mother and I did not have it registered so I was a little anxious about it. So I must close for this time. So good by. Write soon.

From your Sister Louisa Houston to Agnes Houston

Elizabeth Waughtal Houston was the mother of Louisa Houston, wife of Morgan Earp. COURTESY OF LYMAN HANLEY

Poetry for Agnes,

There's not a joy this world can give like it takes it away.
When the glow of early thoughts decline in feelings dwell decay.
'Tis not on youths smooth cheek the blush alone which fades so fast.
But the tender bloom of heart is gone ere youth itself is past.

The following week, Louisa was so excited to spend a little time alone with Morgan that she couldn't wait to share the news in a letter to her sister Kate:

Temescal, San Bernardino,
California
May the 11th
1880

Dear Sister Kate,[45]
Your letter of the 29th is at hand with much welcome for I am indeed very glad to hear from you and I thank you very much for your picture. It is a very good picture but I don't think it looks a bit natural but I knew it was you the moment I put my eyes on it. My husband thinks you are a great deal better looking than me but I can't see the point for I think I look very [well?] to have weathered the storm I have during the past seven years. My face has held it's [sic] own pretty well, you can bet for I have suffered death a thousand times and have often longed for it. Although I can never get well again, I have hopes of getting strong and able to get around like other folks, that is if I live long enough and I begin to think I am going to live about as long as anybody for I guess I am pretty tough after all. Although it is very painful for me to be on my feet much, I manage to get around and do considerable work. Me and

my old man is all alone today for the old folks have gone to town thirty miles away to be gone a week so we are going to have a good time. There is a dance tomorrow night and we are going. I never made much of a success at dancing but I will go. I have been here over two months and have only been off the place once. There is only one boarder at the springs, so there is not much work to do. I haven't anything to write of interest [to?] you so I guess I will have to close for this time. Hoping to hear from you soon. I think Bessie is a very pretty little girl and I think mother's picture is very natural. I don't think she could have a better one taken if she wanted to.

Give my love to all from your Sister Louisa Houston to Kate Houston.

Louisa Houston's sister Catherine "Kate" with husband John Robinson and their children. COURTESY OF LYMAN HANLEY

Although it's not clear what caused Louisa's health to decline beginning around 1873, one of her letters mentions that she suffered from rheumatism. Rheumatism was a somewhat generic medical term that meant swelling and inflammation of various parts of the body. Modern known illnesses such as lupus and fibromyalgia would have fallen under that category in the nineteenth century.

On July 19, 1880, Morgan alone set out to meet his older brothers and their wives in Tombstone, Arizona. Unbeknownst to Morgan, this boomtown chapter would be his last. Right before he left, Louisa penned a letter to her sister:

Temescal, San Bernardino Co.
California
July 19, 1880

Dear Sister Agnes,

Your kind and most welcome letter is at hand. I am very glad to hear from you and to hear you are all well. This has me quite well at present and I sincerely hope when this comes to hand it will find you all enjoying the best of health. I am very obliged to you for the picture. I think it is the very image of you. I was showing it and Kate's to some ladies visitors on Sunday and they called yours the best looking. She used to be when you were girls together but now she takes a much older looking picture. You say you think Bashford's picture is very natural, perhaps it is, but I don't think so. Tell Olive she must hurry up and have that picture taken she promised me. My husband starts for Arizona in the morning. I am going to stay here for the present with his parents. They do not want me to go and I do not want to go so I think I will stay here this summer. We have ripe peaches and watermelons and green corn since the first of the month and we have not had any rain for four months, but we have very pleasant weather. The thermometer has not been above eighty for a month and the most of the time at sixty five and seventy and the nights are very cool.

We cannot sleep without a quilt over us. The nights are very calm and quiet and the days are most always breezy. This is written so badly I don't think you can read it very well. I have no news to write at present so I will close for this time hoping to hear from you very soon. Give my love to all.

From your sister Louisa Houston to Agnes Houston

Louisa's illness had started to affect her handwriting, as she noted to her sister Agnes, and her letters became increasingly hard to decipher. As the summer arrived, Louisa enjoyed her beautiful surroundings, continued to struggle with health issues, and kept in touch with her family by diligently writing letters home.

Temescal Mountains, Cala
August the 30th, 1880

Dear Sister Agnes

Your kind and most welcome letter is at hand. I am very glad to hear from you and to hear that you are all well and that mother's health is improving. My health is about the same, not very much improved. I do not see much improvement as I have had the rumatisism [sic] a great deal lately but I do not mind that much as it has become nature for me to be sick. If I was well, I would not know myself. I think I should run around so much I would make myself sick so it is the same, anyway with me sick or well.

The weather is very pleasant with us although it is quite cool for this time of year but very dry, as we have had no rain since April. My husband is still in Arizona and he writes that it has rained steady there for sixty days during the daytime, but at night it quits. The rail road is washed away in one part of the country is flooded with water, so I suppose it is a great blessing to the poor people to have a little water without paying for it. I believe it is three cents a gallon, not very much but it counts up in the long run. I was up in San Bernardino when your letter came and that was two weeks as it came the day after I left and I stayed two weeks. I went to get my teeth fixed but could not get them fixed there and so I shall have to go to Riverside about twenty miles off. I shall go tomorrow and I dread the ride very much but it is a beautiful little town, the main avenue, as it is called, is eight miles long.

The road is double, two roads running side by side with a row of ornamental trees running between the roads and also on each side is laid out in squares owned by different people. Some owns a great many squares alone. Then there are evergreens and ornamentals trees of every description, then there is fountains, and flower gardens and orchards until you get tired of looking and a great many of these flowers grow on large trees and if their houses are only one story, they will hide them from view.

It is useless for me to attempt to describe anything as it looks, you would think it is paradise if you could only see the beautiful places and I hope you will someday for it is considered one of the prittest [sic] places in southern California. I will try to get some of those acornes [sic] although I cannot get any but old ones and they are not very good and the young acornes [sic] grow so slow it will be a long time before they are ripe and to their final size. So I will close for this time hoping to hear from you all soon. Give my love to all.

From your Sister Louisa Houston to Agnes Houston

By October Louisa had gotten tired of being alone and wished Morgan would send for her.

Sanbernardino [sic]
Sanbernardino County
California
October the 28th, 1880

Dear Sister Agnes,
    Your kind and welcome letter is at hand. I am quite well at present and hope when those few lines come to hand, they will find you all enjoying the best of health although I was very much surprised to hear that you have all gone to Minnesota,[46] especially after Olive and Peter[47] for I hardly thought they would go but I am much pleased to know things have [illegible] for it will be much plesenter [sic] for you all to be near one another, as for me of course you can see by my address that I have not gone to Arizona and perhaps will not go for a month yet but I am living in San Bernardino and will stay here until my husband sends for me to go to Arizona which I hope will not be very long for I am tired enough of the town although it is very pleasant place to live with roses blooming all around and many other flowers that bloom all winter but we are not thinking about yet although it is time for rain. The best flowers do not have any seed, they grow from the roots. I am going to send some seeds to Olive and mother. They can divide them for I suppose Olive will give to herself. I do not know the names of them all for most of the seed was given to me. I have got a few acornes [sic], I will send them to Olive.
    I could not get many and I have a few shells for Bessie. I have been in hopes of going to the shore before I leave but I don't hardly think I will get to go. If I could only get to the cost [sic], I would get you all so many pretty shells. You have no idea how beautiful some of them are, and what curositys [sic].
    As I have not news to interest you, I must close, give my love to all and retain a portion for yourself. So I will bid you good by [sic]

Louisa Houston's sister Elizabeth "Bessie" with husband Lyman Hanley
COURTESY OF LYMAN HANLEY

for the present. Write soon. I remain as ever, your affectionate Sister
Louisa Houston to Agnes Houston
 *Direct your letters to Sanbernardino [*sic*] City, Sanbernardi-*
*noo [*sic*] Co., Cala.*

In all, Louisa ended up waiting five months before being reunited with her husband around December 1, 1880, in Tombstone. Until this time she had signed her letters as Louisa Houston, but Morgan asked her to change that in this letter. Once she arrived in Tombstone, she wrote a somewhat melancholy letter to her sister Agnes:

Tombstone, Cochise County
Arizona
[March 1881, based on her sister's wedding]

Dear Sister Agnes
 After much negligence I at last take my pen in hand to let you know that I am at least alive though not very well although about the same as usual and I hope those few lines will find you well and happy which I am sure you must be. I received a letter from Kate a few days ago stating that you were married[48] on the 13th of last month. Be assured I wish you much joy. You have my earnest congratulations and good wishes for a long surely happy married life. I hope each succeeding year will find you happier than the one before. God bless you and yours and surround you ever with life's choicest blessings. [Illegible] though some of us have our misfortunes and troubles it is a blessing to know that others can be happy. We would not know how to sympathize with the unhappy. It is a good blessing that we have sorrow sometimes during our lives for thus we can appreciate true happiness when it falls to our lot.

I received a letter from Bashford a few days ago and I have answered. It is the first one I have received from him in six months. I have not heard from Olive for a good while. Perhaps it is because I asked her for a picture she has of some of you. I don't know which. Have you got one of my pictures I had taken in Mason City?[49] The first one I ever had taken. If you will send one to me to have one struck off I will return it to you. I want one of them very much.

My husband has promised to send me home on a visit this summer but I shall not put any hope on it until I get started. You must have your husband's picture taken and send me one. I would like to have one very much. We have had a little snow shower, it lay on the ground about two hours. We have had no rain and it is very dry and dusty and the wind blows very hard for the past two weeks except for a few days which was so warm we nearly melted with the doors and windows open. This is like California when the flowers bloom all winter. Some parts of Arizona are quite cold but not here. You asked me who Virgil Earp was. He is an older brother of Morgan's. I sent you some papers that will tell who he is. His name is in both of them. And also Morgan and Wyatt Earp also older. He wishes me to have my letters directed to Louisa Earp so you can direct the next one as so. I will close by sending my love to all and hoping to hear from you very soon.

My best regards to your husband from your Sister Louisa Houston, Mrs. Morgan Earp.

Louisa obliged Morgan by having her letters addressed to Louisa Earp or Mrs. Morgan Earp until July 1881, when she made a direct comment at the close of her July letter to Agnes.

Tombstone, A.T. 1881
July the 19th

Dear Sister Agnes

After some neglect I at last seat myself to answer your kind letter which came to hand some time ago. I am quite well at present. My health has improved a great deal of late. I hope when this comes to hand, it will find you all enjoying the best of health. We are having very disagreeable weather here at present. We have had several hard rains and some terrible hard thunder storms. Our first good shower came on the fourth of July, although it cleared up in the afternoon and was very pleasant and cool, and I went to the Ball, the first one I have been to since I have been in Tombstone. I had a pleasant time. I suppose you go to balls. I do not dance very many dances. I have never been strong enough to dance much, but I do admire fine dancing.

I hope you had a pleasant [illegible]. I am told we will have rain every day steady for two or three months. It rains mostly in the afternoons. We had ripe watermelons here on the fourth. One thing this country is noted for is mocking birds. Most every family has got one or a half dozen, also red birds and blue birds. They all sing. There are a good many parrots here. They are brought in from Mexico by the Mexicans. The singing birds are sold from five to twenty dollars apiece. I don't know how they sell their parrots. I was to their camp today. They had about five hundred birds for sale of different kinds. They camp out and look just like Indians with their shawls over their heads, and they don't speak a word of American if you would pay them for it, but the Mexican language is very easy to learn if any body [sic] tries to learn it. Most all the white children here speak the Mexican language well.

Sister, I am going to ask you a question. I asked you once before and you did not answer it. Have I got any Uncle Waughtals in this part of the continent? If you know anything about them, tell me in your next letter. I have asked all that I write to, and no one of them have answered my question. I begin to think you have some reason for not telling me. So I have nothing of interest to write, and I don't suppose you can read what I have written. It is so poorly done. So I will bid you goodby for this time, and you must write soon. Give my love to all the folks, and accept a share for yourself and husband.

I remain as ever your affectionate Sister
Direct your letters to Louisa Houston

Her next letter home is much like the others where she talked about Tombstone, flowers, and family.

Tombstone, A.T 1881
September the 4th

Dear Sister Agnes

I seat myself to answer your kind and most welcome letter which came a few days ago.

I am very glad you are well and happy. I am about as well as usual. Your letter was delayed by the road being flooded out. We have had some very hard rains and there has been big wash outs, both east and west, but I believe the roads are all right now. I went to the mountains and stayed a week, but I did not get any cactuses. There were none there like I wanted to get. I will send you a piece of

California Liveforever that my sister in law[50] sent me from California, also some sprouts of verbinia [sic] and borgement [sic]. It does not have a pretty blossom it is only for its sweet smell. I got them through the mail in a little box. I will send them to you the same way. If they are not delayed, they will grow I think. I don't know how that letter ever came to be sent to the dead letter office. I go to the post office every week. It certainly was the postmaster's carelessness. I think those roses are very pretty. I will send you some pressed verbinia [sic] leaves, they have pretty foliage and make a pretty house plant and will grow all winter if they do not freeze. The leaves are spotted. They are yellow at first but fades white when it grows older. Well our city is in a big excitement at present, the Indians are on the war path all around us and have killed a great many people.

The people here expect to be attacked any day. Some of them are terribly afraid, but I think the place is too large to be taken easily and there are three forts within forty and fifty miles of Tombstone. There was no passenger train in Benson today. I hear they are kept to bring in soldiers. The news only came in last night of the Indians, but of course it is exaggerated, at least we all hope so.

So I will close for this time, give my love to all the folks and accept a portion for yourself and husband.

I remain as ever your affectionate Sister.

Direct mail to Louisa Houston

I have not forgotten you promised me a picture of yourself and husband. I will send you a Tombstone paper Sept. the 5th, this mornings. The rain is pouring down in torrents. I will send you a piece of my hair in this and a piece for Olive.

Tombstone, A. G. _____ 1881

Sept the 4th

Dear Sister Agnes

I seat my self to answer your kind and most welcom letter which came to hand a few days ago I am very glad you are well and happy I am about as well as usual your letter was delayed by the road being flooded out we have had some very hard rains and there has been big wash outs both east and west but I believe the roads are all right now I went out to the mountains and stayed a week but I did not get any cactus there was none there likes I wanted to get I will send you a price of california fireforever that my sisterinlaw sent me from california also some sprouts of verbenia and bergemant it does not have a pritty blossom it is only for the sweet smell I got them through the mail in a little box I will send them you the same way, if they are not delayed they will grow think I dont know how that letter ever came to be it to the dead letter office I goto the post office every week it certainly was the post masters carelisness. I think those roses are very pritty I will send you some pressed verbenia

This is Louisa's original September 4, 1881, letter. COURTESY OF LYMAN HANLEY

coming they bear a very pretty foliage and enclosure pretty begonia
last and will grow all winter if they do not freeze the
ours are spotted they are yellow at first but fade white when
grows older   well our city is in a big excitement
& present the indians are on the war path all around
& and have killed a great many people the people
in expect to be stated every day some of them are terribly afraid
of & think the place is to large to be taken easily and
there are store forts within forty and fifty miles of tombstone
there was no passenger train in benson today I hear they are
kept to bring in soldiers the news only come in last night of the
indians but of corse it is exagerated at least we all pope so. so I will.
close for this time give my love to all the folks and except a potion for your
self and husband I remain as ever your affectionate sister to Loving Houston

I have not forgotten you promised me a picture of your self and husbar
I will send you a tombstone papers ° (Sept th 5 th this morning
the rain is poring down in torrents
I will send you a peice of my dress in this
and a piece for Idim

Her next two letters were written after the gunfight in October and Virgil's assassination attempt. By this time, all of the Earps had moved into the Cosmopolitan Hotel.

Tombstone, A.T.
Cochise Co.
Jan. the 31st, 1882

Dear Sister

Your kind and welcome letter came to hand this evening. I thought I would not neglect it as I did the one before. Your thought-ful [illegible].

Started to California last week but have given up the notion all together. I think it is best to stay with my husband in trouble. He wants me to go to his fathers to stay the rest of the winter. They are good old fashioned people and very kind to me when I was with them. I lived with them eight months, and could not have been treated better if I was their own daughter. I am much healthier now than when I first came to Arizona. I do not like you to feel [illegible] coming year as it has in the past six months. I shall then come home on visit although my husband has promised to let me go last summer, and this winter, he always changes his mind before the time arrives for me to start, fearing I will take sick while away.

Feb. the 4th

I did not finish this on the 31st. I was waiting for the weather to clear up to have a picture taken. We have had several light snows [illegible] the night, and melts during the day. So it is very muddy at [illegible].

There has been some sleighing at Colton, California about a month ago. That has never been known there before. So I will close for this time. Hope to hear from you soon. Give my love to all.

From your Sister Louisa Houston

Any letter that is not directed in this name is always opened by my husbands brothers. Tomorrow first passenger train ten miles distant [illegible] be one of the first letters that goes out on the [illegible] from that [illegible].

Tell Agnes to not [illegible] on me as soon as I am settled again I will write a good long letter. I forgot to say that ever since our trouble we have been living in the Cosmopolitan Hotel, and it is very disagreeable to be so unsettled.

It's curious as to why they would open any of her letters in the first place, but to choose only the ones addressed to her as Mrs. Earp is especially peculiar. Louisa then wrote another letter on February 4 that goes into more detail about Virgil's assassination attempt.

February the 4th, 1882

[Illegible] under any obligation for what little I have done for you. I am only sorry it is so little. It will always be a pleasure to me to feel I can be of any help to you. I will try to find that piece in the paper and send it to you. Do you piece quilts? I mean all of you,[51] Agnes, mama, Aunt Helen and Susan. If you would like to have some quilt pieces, I will send them. I have sent Olive a few. I sent her word I was going away for a few days.

[Illegible] yet awhile. I will send you my picture. [illegible] uncle Bill and aunt Helen and tell them I would like their picture very much. I believe uncle Bill has one of my pictures I had taken in Mason City. Please tell him if he will send it to me to have one struck off it, I will return it to him with many thanks. It has been taken about ten years ago. I would like to see if I have changed so very much. I imagine my sickness has made me grow old very fast. If my health improves as much in the [illegible].

Virgil was shot about a month ago. He was also shot the same time Morgan was shot, but only slightly. It is quite impossible to tell You [sic] all the trouble and anxiety it has caused us, so I will not attempt to.

[Illegible] wise occupied. I am sorry to say was only too true. My husband was wounded. He was shot through both shoulders, both shoulder blades were broken and the spinal column was slightly injured, but he has quite recovered and has been out in the country for the past week. I have sent Agnes our weekly paper. We have two weekly and two daily papers. The Epitaph *is our friend and the* Nugget, *it has so many falsehoods in it you would almost feel like doubting the other paper. My husband's brother Virgil Earp is not expected to recover.*

After the attempted assassination attempt on Virgil, the Earps cautiously went about their business, but at 10:50 p.m. on March 18, 1882, another tragic event happened.

Despite warnings from many in town, Morgan went to Schieffelin Hall to watch *Stolen Kisses* performed by the Lingard Troupe. After the show he headed toward Campbell & Hatch's Saloon and Billiard Parlor. His brother Wyatt met him on the street in front of the saloon. As Wyatt approached Morgan, he said, "It's just a hunch, Morg, but I want you to come along to the hotel and go to bed." Morgan said, "I want to have one game of pool with Bob Hatch. I promised I would play a game. It won't take that long. Then I'll go to bed." Prior to this conversation, Wyatt had been undressing in his room at the Cosmopolitan Hotel when a premonition of trouble caused him to get dressed and find his younger brother.[52]

Wyatt followed Morgan into the pool hall and watched as his younger brother walked to the pool table in the back. Morgan and Hatch began playing pool on newly covered tables. Wyatt rested on a chair sitting against the wall halfway down the room. Still feeling an uneasiness he could never describe, he got up and moved to a chair in the back of the pool room, near Morgan.

With Bob Hatch watching carefully, Morgan leaned over to make a difficult shot, with his back to the door. At that moment, two bullets, fired in rapid succession, crashed through the glass panel doors in the back of the saloon. Through the smoke, Wyatt watched as Morgan slipped to the floor. As he fell, Morgan tried to remove his gun from his holster but was too weak. Wyatt ran to Morgan's side and asked, "Are you badly hurt, Morg?" Morgan replied, "Not badly, I guess." He looked down at his feet and said to Wyatt, "Take off my shoes, Wyatt." Wyatt took his shoes off, knowing Morgan did not want to die with his boots on. "Lay me straight, Wyatt." Wyatt just looked at him and said, "You are straight, Morgan. Just as straight as you can be." Morgan said, "Then my back is broken." He was correct, as the bullet had entered on the right side of his abdomen and passed through his spinal column, completely shattering it. The second shot had just missed Wyatt, passing over his head and lodging in the wall near the saloon's ceiling.

Morgan was carried to the card room in the saloon and placed on a lounge chair. Meanwhile, his brothers Wyatt, Virgil, James, and Warren, along with Virgil and James's wives and a few intimate friends, were sent for and rushed to his side. It's most likely Louisa was back in California with Morgan's parents when he was killed, since she was not mentioned. They tried to get Morgan to his feet, but he said, "Don't, I can't stand it. This is the last game of pool I'll ever play."[53]

From half past eleven until midnight, Morgan's mind was clear, and he spoke to his brothers Wyatt, James, and Warren. Morgan asked Wyatt if he knew who had shot him. Wyatt told him he did and that he would get them. Morgan replied, "That's all I'll ask, but Wyatt, be careful." Just after midnight, and on March 19, Wyatt's birthday, his brother passed away. Later that day, Morgan's body was sent home to Colton, California, with his older brother James as an escort.[54]

There has been some controversy over whether Louisa was in Tombstone when Morgan was killed. Louisa made a curious statement that makes it appear she was not in Tombstone: "Do you ever hear from our uncles in Arizona? They lived at Dos Cabezas, a small mining camp fifteen miles off the railroad. I heard one of them came to Tombstone for me after my husband was killed, but I was in California at the time." One could take this to mean that either she was in California at the time of his murder, or she was in Tombstone when he was killed, but left after his death and before her uncle arrived. More clues that she may have been in California are the newspaper accounts of Morgan's death, which never mention her. One final item that makes it appear as though she had left Tombstone before her husband's murder is the fact that that her name was listed in the *Daily Epitaph* on February 25, 1882, under the unclaimed letter list. Additionally, a note in the *Los Angeles Herald* indicates she was not in Tombstone at the time: "James Earp, one of the famous Earp brothers, was in Los Angeles yesterday, and will remain a few days. He came down from Colton, to which point he had accompanied the body of his deceased brother, Morgan." It may mention only James because he came to Los Angeles alone, and the newspaper reporter did not know who may or may not have been with James in Colton. Researcher Kenneth Vail states, "There was an express train out of LA that bypassed the majority of regular stops. From LA the stops were Colton (all trains stopped at Colton) then all the way to Yuma. This is how Louisa could rendezvous with Jim and Morg's body, by going only as far as Yuma. Jim coming the opposite way would naturally stop at Yuma. And sure enough the Yuma papers made a pointed announcement about how Morgan Earp had passed by their town on Monday. In other words, there must have been pertinent conversation at the Yuma depot. Therefore the scenario would fit with what Adelia Earp Edwards (Morgan's sister) said about Lou flying off in desperation to be with Morg's body. She didn't have to go all the way to Tucson to accomplish that."

Additionally, during a 1934 interview Morgan's sister, Adelia, claimed Louisa was not in Tombstone when Morgan was killed "and we used to wonder about Morgan's wife, too. When she heard he had been murdered, she went off to Arizona to bring his body back to Colton and only stayed with us a few weeks more after he was put to rest. She was a real sad lady. I recall best that sad look in her eyes. But she was a fine person and a stunning looker, and she was waiting for Morg to come back from Tombstone when she heard. She just fell down on the floor and sobbed and sobbed. She lived in Tombstone a short time, but Morg sent her home to wait until they were ready to come home. I guess he was worried for her there. She was a clever young lady, had been to good schools. She just went away. We just don't know what became of her."[55]

Louisa penned a letter to a friend named Budd Davis, who lived in Butte, Montana, and was a boardinghouse owner and sporting man. She wrote this letter on Morgan's funeral card that she sent to him.

Colton, California
March the 22nd, 1882

From Mrs. Morgan Earp
To Budd Davis

His father dispached [sic] for his body to be sent home for burial. It was sent on the 19th and was buried on the 21st he was shot in the back the ball passing entirley [sic] through the body breaking the spinal column he was shot through the back door of billiard room the door was glass he was shot at 11 o'clock at night and died at 12 living one hour he died with a smile on his face he did not talk very much but he looked around at his brothers smiled and said it was very hard to die that way—for you know well Budd that Morgan Earp was a brave man as ever lived and he was cruely [sic] murdered without a single chance for his life or a moments warning and he died without a complaint or moan but smiled pleasantly which plainly shoud [sic] he was not afraid of death. I have often heard him say that he would willingly lay down his own life to save any of his brothers and I am more content when I think it is just as he would have it be if he could speak and tell us his wishes. I am living with his parents at Colton oh Budd it is so hard to give up the dearest of all earth. I could give him up any other way and still had hopes. But death there is no disputing

This photograph of Louisa's family in Minnesota was taken around 1890. Her brother Robert is the tall man next to the horses, her sister Elizabeth is behind the bike, and her mother, Elizabeth Waughtal Houston, is standing to the right of the baby buggy. COURTESY OF LYMAN HANLEY

118

no bringing back he was so generous so charitable he has always had so many friends. God is to [sic] just to let his murderes [sic] go unpunished who ever [sic] they are we do not know as soon as I get the papers with the account of every particular of the sad affair I will send them to you please have it copied in the Butte papers if possible and I will be greatful [sic]. From your bereaved and sorrowing friend Mrs Louisa Alice Earp.

After Morgan's death she visited her family in Minnesota and then returned to California. She eventually married again on New Year's Eve in 1885 to Henry Gustav Peters. Her next letter was to tell her sister Agnes about her marriage.

Los Angeles, California
Feb. the 3rd, 1886

Dear Sister
    After my long neglect, I at last seat myself to write a few lines home. I am in very good health at the present and I hope this will find you all the same. I have forgotten Olive's address, if you will send it to me, I would like to write to her. My husband will send you a few lines also. I was married on New Years Eve.[56] I will send mama some of the wedding cake. I think there will be a little for all of you if it does not get smashed all to pieces in the mail. I have lived in Los Angeles since last April. It is a beautiful place, the oranges are just nice and ripe now and most of the roses and lilies are in bloom now. Do you ever hear from our uncles[57] in Arizona? They lived at Dos Cabezas a small mining camp fifteen miles off the railroad. I heard one of them came to Tombstone for me after my husband was killed, but I was in California at the time. I shall not write very much this time. My husband writes Papa and

Henry Gustav Peters married Louisa Houston after her husband, Morgan Earp, was murdered. COURTESY OF LYMAN HANLEY

Mama a letter also with my best love to all. I will close hoping to hear from you very soon.

From your affectionate sister Louisa Peters

Her new husband apparently wanted to be liked by her sister Agnes, so he penned her a letter just two days after they were married. He began, "I have won the hand and heart of your Dear Sister Louisa. I am since December 31st, 1885, her true and lawful husband. Consequently, your brother-in-law, and as such I beg you to hold good will towards me. I am poor in worldly goods, but if a God fearing true heart is to be accounted as a good gift, I shall for a lifetime be the good and faithful husband of the best and noblest woman, my own sweet little wife Louisa."

Less than nine years into the marriage, Peters wrote this letter to Louisa's sister Agnes:

Although a stranger, allow me to address you as your brother-in-law. To be short in my explanation, I, Henry G. Peters, married your sister Louisa on the 31st of December 1885, in Los Angeles through the Rev. G. Dorsey, Minister of the Gospel. We have been very happy during our married life, which ended on the 12th June 1894. My dear Lou was attacked with Sciatic Reheumatism [sic] for the last three years to which Dropsy added itself at ending her sufferings of the above date. I have written to father and mother asking their blessings, but never received a reply, but whatever our human feelings, they certainly should have forgiven her, because my dear Lou was always a good wife and helpmate to me. . . . But permit me to extend to you my best wishes and heartfelt wishes. Keep up courage. We do not know what good there is in store for us, and as this letter reaches you, please answer it immediately. I shall be a true friend and help as far as it in my power towards you. Kiss your

children for me and accept the best wishes for your brother-in-law.
H. G. Peters. Please write soon and give mother my address. Love
and esteem. H. G. Peters, Long Beach, Ca.

He later wrote, "Then dear Louisa was attacked with Scyatic [*sic*]
Rheumatisme [*sic*], and although I sent her to Elsinore and Temescal
Hot Springs, she never got well, but kept ailing on and off until the last
three years where she was almost a confirmed cripple, until it pleased
God to relieve her of her suffering. God rest her!!!"

Gustav alludes to the fact that Louisa's parents had either dis-
owned her or were mad at her for something. Could it be she ran off
when she was under eighteen and took her younger sister with her?
Further illumination on this theory comes from another of Peters's
letters to Louisa's mother, Elizabeth, "regarding dear departed Louisa,
Godd [*sic*] in his infinite mercy relieved her of all her severe sufferings
and given her rest, so dear mother do not grieve but take through me
her last loving words and goodby with the hope of meeting her at the
throne of mercy—where there is no parting."

Gustav was rather friendly with a sister-in-law he'd never met,
continuing to send Agnes letters professing his willingness to care for
her and her children—in fact, almost begging her and her mother to
accept his help. Then abruptly, after he remarried he cooled to sister-
in-law Agnes:

Mrs. Agnes Cebell, Your rather inquisitive and unwarranted let-
ter at hand. As I am married again since three months, I have a
good wife and boy to care for. Consequently no time to correspond. I
have done my duty towards your dear sister and have to labor yet to
straighten matters financially, and as I am even now on the sick list.
I have more duty to fulfill than to waste time in writing. In regard
to your sister's clothes, it is unreasonable to send as they are rather

worse for appearance first, and secondly, the freight to your place is too high. Wishing you all well, I am H. G. Peters.

When Louisa Earp died on June 12, 1894, she was thirty-nine. She's buried alone in the Evergreen Cemetery in Los Angeles, California, where her grave was originally marked as Mrs. L. Peters. Around 2003 a new headstone was put on her grave by historians Tom Gaumer and Kenneth Vail, reading, "Mrs. Louisa Houston Earp Peters."

This photo was taken in 1930. Standing, left to right, are Louisa Houston's sisters Catherine, Elizabeth, and Agnes; their mother, Elizabeth, is seated.
COURTESY OF LYMAN HANLEY

Chapter Four

Mr. & Mrs. James Earp

"Mr. Earp is accompanied here by his wife, a very beautiful brunette."

—*LA Daily Times*, March 28, 1882

Although James Earp was with his more well-known brothers all over the West, history rarely remembers him because he was not involved in the street fight in Tombstone. James "Jim" Cooksey Earp was born June 24, 1841, in Hartford, Kentucky, and was the first son of Nicholas Porter and Victoria "Virginia" Ann Cooksey-Earp. By the time he was nine his parents had moved to Lake Prairie, Iowa, and then on to Pella by 1860. James grew to be five feet, eight inches and had blue eyes and light hair. While living in Pella he was a stagecoach driver. The *LA Daily Times* described him as being of stout build with a heavy moustache.

On May 25, 1861, this nineteen-year-old farm boy traveled to Peoria, Illinois, where he enlisted as a private in Captain Josiah Moore's Company F, 17th Illinois Infantry Regiment. He donned the Union Blue and was supposed to serve for three years but was injured shortly after enlisting. On October 21, 1861, he was shot from behind through his left shoulder at the battle of Fredericktown, Missouri. The bullet passed through the shoulder, hit the joint, and exited through the breastbone. He was hospitalized for his injury and while he recovered,

James Cooksey Earp was the eldest son of Nicholas and Virginia Ann. He was a Civil War veteran and lost the use of his left arm during the war.
COURTESY OF ROBERT G. MCCUBBIN

he was not able to use his left arm. The US Army discharged him on March 22, 1863, citing that he could not use a musket and he would not recover the use of his arm. He went home.

After returning to Marion County, Iowa, James crossed the Plains with his family as they headed to California in 1864. He split from the family and traveled to Austin, Nevada, and then headed to the Northwest, where from 1865 to 1870 he lived in Idaho City and Boise, Idaho Territory; Walla Walla, Washington Territory; Cheyenne, Wyoming Territory; and Helena and Deer Lodge, Montana Territory. His sister, Adelia, recalled Jim's love of the West in a 1934 interview: "Jim just loved Montana and the north. He spent many years up there. For many years of his life he was in Montana at different times from a young man until he settled down here. . . . He would talk of Butte, Deadwood, Seattle, Salt Lake City, and he and Bessie had a set of real fine pictures made in Leadville, Colorado. All the boys had been most everywhere."

In 1871 James left the boomtowns for Pineville, Missouri; a year later he traveled to his father's farm in Aullville, Missouri, where he met up with his brothers Wyatt and Morgan. In 1872 James ventured to Newton and Kansas City, Kansas, and then back to Missouri. On May 30, 1873, he was issued a land patent for 145 acres from the government in the town of Boonville, Missouri.

In 1873 James married Bessie Nellie Bartlett Catchim. This mysterious Mrs. Earp was born in New York around 1841, but to whom is uncertain. There's been some question about the spelling of her last name, and a letter addressed to her daughter, Hattie B., shows Outchim, but it's likely a misspelling. There is, however, documentation that indicates she had two children: a son named Frank and a daughter named Hattie (short for Harriett) B. Catchim. Also, it can be concluded that Bessie was married to a man named Catchim before marrying James, because her daughter, Hattie, is listed with a variation of that name in the 1880 Tombstone census as James's stepdaughter.

To date, there is no documentation available that would provide any other indisputable details about Bessie. The interchangeable use of her names Bessie and Nellie further complicates any attempts to discern her legal first name, since Bessie is a common nineteenth-century nickname for Elizabeth, and Nellie is a nickname for Eleanor or Helen. There may also be some confusion as to her maiden name, which is Bartlett, according to James's pension records. It's possible that neither Bartlett nor Catchim was her maiden name, and they instead were both married names.

There is a household listed in the 1870 US census that *could* include Bessie. At the time of the census, a family in Knoxville, Marion County, Iowa, consisted of a D. Bartlett, age forty-four; an E. E. Bartlett, (which could be Elizabeth Eleanor), age twenty-nine; a J. E. Bartlett, age thirteen; an F. D. Bartlett (which could be Frank), age eleven; and an H. B. (which could be Hattie B.), age seven. All were born in New York, and E. E., F. D., and H. B. are the correct ages to be Bessie and her two known children. It's possible that Catchim could have been a first husband who died in the war or otherwise, and that she then remarried D. Bartlett, and the children went by his name in the census. However, without first names, there is no certainty this household listed in the census was Bessie's.

According to James Earp, he and Bessie were married on April 18, 1873, in Illinois by a justice of the peace, but he couldn't remember any other details. He also stated that her maiden name was Nellie Bartlett and that she had married a man named Ketchum, who died before she married James. A year later Jim and Bessie made their way to Wichita, Kansas, where Bessie was listed as a "sporting" girl. In early May 1874 Bessie, or as the sheriff's report cited her, "Betsy," and Wyatt's wife, "Sally" (Sallie), were each fined $8 for prostitution. On June 3, 1874,

Bessie and Sallie were arrested again for keeping a brothel and pleaded guilty to the charge. Since they did not have the $250 for bail money, they were locked up. They eventually got the money and were released and their case was dismissed. Bessie continued to be fined off and on for prostitution until March 1875. Curiously, while she and James were listed as living in Wichita, they were at different addresses. Her children, Frank and Hattie, ages fifteen and twelve, respectively, were not listed in that census, nor could they be found in any other records at this time.

After living for a couple years in Wichita, it appears Bessie and James traveled to Troy, Kansas, where in 1876 James was granted a

This is believed to be Bessie Catchim Bartlett, who was James Earp's common-law wife.
GLENN BOYER COLLECTION, COURTESY OF SCOTT DYKE

government land patent. Between 1877 and 1878, James was a bartender in Fort Worth at 47 Main Street and then at 9th and Calhoun at the Cattle Exchange Saloon. In late 1879 they arrived in Prescott, Arizona Territory, with Bessie's daughter, Hattie, along with Wyatt and Mattie, to join Virgil and strike out to the silver boomtown of Tombstone, Arizona. James, Bessie, and Hattie settled into a home on Fremont Street, and James got a job dealing faro and then as a bartender at Vogan's Bowling Alley Saloon. Regarding James, Allie Earp recalled, "Everybody gambled and he was always liked as a square gambler that never got into fusses like Wyatt, or Virge either."

The June 2, 1880, US census lists Bessie Earp with James C. and Hattie Earp (as his daughter) on Allen Street in Tombstone. However, Hattie B. was his stepdaughter and her last name was still legally Catchim. On June 3, 1880, the federal government finally got all those details correct. For some reason, James, Bessie, and Hattie were counted twice in the 1880 US census.

February 3, 1881, was quite an eventful day for Hattie: She celebrated not only her eighteenth birthday, but also her wedding, marrying Thaddeus Stephens Harris, who owned the Tombstone Foundry and Machine Shop. The marriage was not a happy one for Hattie; in February 1889 she was visiting San Francisco and sent him a letter stating she wished to end their marriage. In November 1889 Thaddeus Harris filed a suit against his wife, Hattie B. Harris, for desertion. They were divorced and in 1890 she married the successful cattleman William Land.[58]

While Hattie stayed in Tombstone with her husband, Thaddeus Harris, her mother left. After Morgan was killed in 1882, Bessie and Wyatt's wife, Mattie, boarded a train and headed for the Earp family home in Colton, California. James later joined Bessie. By March 1883 James was tending bar in Colton, California, an occupation where his lame left arm was not a hindrance. Jumping back into the mining circuit, James and Bessie joined his brother Wyatt and his wife up in Coeur d'Alene, Idaho Territory, in 1884. They registered at the St. Charles Hotel in September. By the summer of 1886 they were residing in San Bernardino, where James was a member of the Anti-Riparian Club, which dealt with water rights in the area.

The life of Bessie's son, Frank, is also somewhat of a mystery. Aside from his testimony at his sister Hattie's divorce hearing, not much remains of him. He is listed in the Cochise County (Arizona) Great Register in 1886, which confirms the spelling of his last name as Catchim.

When men registered to vote, they logged their names alphabetically, by last name; Frank is listed in the "C" section with the name Frank Catchim. According to the voting registry, Frank was a twenty-seven-year-old rancher living in Charleston, Arizona, when he registered on September 27, 1886. It's more than likely that the correct spelling of his last name was Catchim, but census enumerators and newspaper reporters often spelled names the way they sounded, so Catchim translated on paper to Ketchum, which was more common.

According to newspaper accounts, Frank Catchim was murdered by Apache Indians on June 3, 1891, near the Oso Negro mine where he was driving a team of freight wagons for J. E. Durkee. One report claims he was shot while making breakfast for himself and the other members of the team; according to the other account, he was feeling ill and rested against a tree, where he was shot in the head. The *Epitaph* reported, "This time it is a Tombstone boy. . . . Catchum was a young man about 27 years of age." Noting someone as a "Tombstone boy" was not uncommon, since many who lived in Charleston often visited Tombstone or swapped between the two towns. It appears the newspaper guessed his age, because if this is the same Frank Catchim, then he would have been thirty or thirty-one years old when he died. James Earp noted in his pension records that Hattie was born in June 1875, which is not at all correct, and Frank was noted as being born in February 1874. If those dates were correct, then James would have been their father, which is not true either. It's odd he also wrote in his pension records that they were both deceased, when in fact, Hattie was very much alive.

James's sister, Adelia, in her 1934 interview, said, "I heard many of the tales from Jim and Bessie in the 1880s after they had come back from Arizona. Bessie was not a happy woman then and it affected her health. She died in a few years, and I reckon her poor heart was broke, what with her daughter running off like that in Tombstone, and then she never knowing what became of her for a long time." Bessie Earp died on January 22, 1887, in San Bernardino of an abscess. She was buried in the Pioneer Cemetery on January 23, 1887, next to her mother-in-law, Virginia Ann Cooksey-Earp. About a year after Bessie's death, James was running a saloon.

In true Earp fashion, he did not remain alone after Bessie died—at least it appears that way. A newspaper article shows a Mr. and Mrs. J.C. Earp set sail for Nome, Alaska, on May 25, 1900. It's likely this is James, since Wyatt and his wife, Josephine, were living and working in Alaska at the time. The 1900 US census also shows there was a J. Earp and H.J. Earp on board the SS *Charles D. Lane*. The ship left San Francisco on June 2, 1900, and arrived in Nome, Alaska, on June 21, 1900. Beyond those scant records, the identity of the second Mrs. James Earp remains a mystery.

James died on January 25, 1926, in Los Angeles. He is buried in the Mountain View Cemetery in San Bernardino, which is the same cemetery where his sister, Adelia, and sister-in-law Allie are buried.

CHAPTER FIVE

Mr. & Mrs. Warren Earp

"[Warren] said that was the last time that he would ever get into trouble over a woman."

—YUMA SENTINEL, NOVEMBER 25, 1893

Warren Baxter Earp was the youngest of the Earp brothers and is rarely mentioned with the Earp brothers. Since he was so much younger than his brothers James, Virgil, and Wyatt, he stayed with his parents while they traversed the West. He did make his way to Tombstone, but not until after the infamous gunfight that made the Earps forever part of Tombstone's history.

He was born March 9, 1855, in Iowa, fourteen years after his older brother James. His family moved from Pella, Iowa, to Lamar, Missouri, before he was old enough to attend school. Just like his brothers, Warren was a restless youth who moved often, following his brothers and parents. He grew to be five feet, ten inches, and had a fair complexion, blue eyes, and light brown hair.

Also like his brothers, Warren had a fondness for racehorses; in 1876 he owned a particularly beloved horse named Selim. His sister-in-law Allie remembered how much he loved his horse: "Warren thought more of that fast-steppin' saddle horse than anything in the world. He entered her in every race he heard of."

Warren Earp, the youngest of the Earp brothers, posed for this photograph circa the 1880s, when he was about twenty-five years old.

Warren was living with his parents in Colton, California, when the infamous October 26, 1881, Cowboys vs. Earps gunfight took place, but he soon joined his brothers in Tombstone. After Morgan's assassination, Warren joined Wyatt in his Vendetta to avenge the murder of their brother. By 1882, when Warren was twenty-seven, he and his brothers Wyatt and Virgil were running a faro game in San Francisco, and in November 1882, Warren was residing in San Francisco on Pine Street with his brothers.

It must have been difficult for Warren, whose brothers had been lawmen, served in the Civil War, and had their names in newspapers. While his brothers were carving out their futures, for better or worse, Warren was at home with Mom and Dad.

Like most young men, Warren no doubt wanted to prove himself to his older brothers. He did manage to get his name in the paper often, but for all the wrong reasons. His quick temper and bad-boy attitude got him in trouble and would be the end of young Warren.

By May 1883 Warren's older brother James had opened a saloon in Colton where Warren got into a quarrel with a Mexican named Belarde who lived nearby. The *Sacramento Daily Record-Union* reported, "It seems Belarde first struck Earp and ran for the door, Earp firing at his target but missing his mark. Earp was at once seized by Deputy Sheriff Adams, who, calling to his assistance others, after a violent struggle, succeeded in wrestling his revolvers from him. But Adams was unable to handcuff Earp, who made his escape after a long struggle, concealing himself from the officers probably to make his escape at night. As Belarde was leaving town about 5 o'clock yesterday afternoon, on horseback, he was pursued by Earp and fired at, there being nine shots exchanged, but at such a range that none took effect. Belarde was arrested by Deputy Sheriff Brown, and while this was being done Earp made his escape from town on a horse."

In April 1884 Warren was in San Bernardino, and according to the *San Jose Evening News,* he entered a restaurant and nearly beat a waiter to death. By October of that year, he was back running a faro game on the notorious Morton Street, now known as Maiden Lane, in San Francisco, but was shut down during a raid in early November.[59] Morton Street was described by author Herbert Asbury in 1933.[60]

The worst cribs in San Francisco were probably those which lined both sides of Morton Street (Maiden Lane). . . . These dens were occupied by women of all colors and nationalities; there were even a few Chinese and Japanese girls. And not only were the Morton Street cribs the lowest in San Francisco's red light district; they were also the most popular, partly because of the great variety and extraordinary depravity of the women to be found there, and partly because the police seldom entered the street unless compelled to do so by a murder or a serious shooting or stabbing affray. Ordinary fights and assaults were ignored. . . .

Every night, and especially every Saturday night, this dismal bedlam of obscenity, lighted only by the red lamps above the doors of the cribs, was thronged by a tumultuous mob of half-drunken men, who stumbled from crib to crib, greedily inspecting the women as if they had been so many wild animals in cages.

Warren apparently then joined his brothers Wyatt and James as they made their way up to the Northwest in early 1884 where his older brothers opened a saloon in Eagle City, Idaho. Even though Wyatt and James soon left, Warren stayed behind until March 1885, when he moved to Spokane Falls, Washington Territory. The hot-tempered Warren got into an altercation with a former business partner, who went unnamed in the newspaper story, and shot him through the hand. When Warren made his way back to the Dingle area of Idaho

Territory in 1887, it appears his stay there may have been more than just mining-related. It was here that he married his first and only known wife, Kate Sanford, at the age of thirty-two. Although it's possible he married before, no records have been located to prove this.

There is, however, evidence of his marriage on June 14, 1887, to Kate Sanford. It's interesting to note that the marriage wasn't recorded until January 21, 1888. Kate lived in Montpelier, Idaho Territory, and the couple was married at the home of Joseph Lewis Jr., who was justice of the peace in Dingle. The marriage record, which is a piece of paper signed by the justice of the peace, lists only the names of the bride, the groom, and the justice of the peace. One Idaho historian did note it was strange there were no witnesses listed on the marriage record.

It's possible that the man listed on this marriage certificate is a different Warren Earp, but the youngest Earp was in Idaho during 1883 and 1884 with his brothers, so it's very likely this is his record. However, without a middle initial, a connecting witness to the marriage, or parents' names, there is no way to confirm with absolute certainty this man was Warren Baxter Earp. However, no other Warren Earp could be found in this area in research records.

Unfortunately, the only details known about Kate Sanford are her name and town of residence. Research revealed a Kate Sanford, born in England about 1855, living with her parents in Salt Lake City, Utah, according to the 1870 census. Her age would be the same as Warren's, but there is no way to know whether it's the same Kate Sanford. Their marriage record is the only piece of evidence of Mrs. Warren Earp. Just what happened to Kate Sanford Earp is another Earp-wife mystery.

By 1892 Warren was back in San Bernardino and listed himself as a capitalist in his voter registration request. In August 1893 he was again in trouble with the law for stabbing Charles Steele. On August 15 about two o'clock in the afternoon, Warren and Steele had been drinking together in Anderson and Beam's Saloon in San Bernardino.

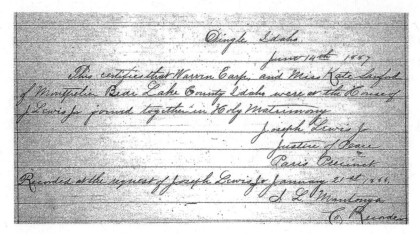

Warren Earp married Kate Sanford in Idaho Territory. This certificate is the only proof she existed.
COURTESY OF BRIGHAM YOUNG UNIVERSITY-IDAHO FAMILY HISTORY CENTER

When Warren called Steele a dirty name, Steele invited him to settle the issue outside. Once outside, Steele threw a punch that hit Warren in the mouth, which caused him to bleed. Warren, who the *Los Angeles Herald* reported was crippled in one hand, responded by drawing a large knife from his hip pocket. He lunged at Steele and stuck him across the back, leaving a four-inch-wide gash. Earp was arrested and taken to the police station, where he was charged with assault with a deadly weapon. Steele recovered. Warren was later released because it was determined Steele started the altercation.[61]

Apparently wearing out his welcome and embarrassing his parents, Warren headed back to Arizona. On November 11, 1893, he was arrested in Yuma for assaulting a man named Professor Behrens. He did not teach as a professor, but was called that because it was a term given to bartenders of the day. It's possible this "professor" Behrens is the same deputy city marshal John Behrens who worked with Wyatt in Wichita. Behrens ran O'Toole's Opera House in town and on his way home from dinner, Warren asked Behrens to walk across a bridge with him, but Behrens refused. Somehow Warren got the professor on the bridge, grabbed him by the throat, and attempted to toss him over, but Behrens held on so Warren couldn't toss him off. Warren then threatened Behrens and demanded the professor pay him to leave town. Behrens didn't have the $100 Warren wanted, but finally escaped after he said he would get Warren $25 after he saw his boss, Mr. Comstock.

As Warren went to pack, Behrens got an officer to arrest Warren when he came to get his money. Warren did not have the bail money, so he was left in jail. The *Yuma Sentinel* wrote, "It is said Earp brought a woman here with him, and that on account of ill treatment she left him. He accuses the Professor of being the cause of her leaving. This is the statement made by Prof. Behrens, who is well-known here." Unfortunately, no records exist that would reveal whether that woman was his wife, Kate, or someone else. Later that month the charge of attempted murder was dismissed because of jurisdiction issues. The paper reported Warren was on the bridge where the Arizona/California state line was, so technically he was in California. Nevertheless, the charge of extortion was still valid since that incident happened in Yuma. Because he didn't have the money to pay the fine, he was put on street detail. After he fulfilled his service, the *Sentinel* again reported, "He promised that he would leave town on the first train which he did. No man has left Yuma for years that was more pleased to get away. While in jail he was most penitent and said that was the last time that he would ever get into trouble over a woman."[62] By January 1895 Warren had secured a position driving a stage in Arizona Territory between Willcox and Fort Grant.

In the winter of 1899, Warren's older brother Virgil made a prediction about his future to his daughter Nellie. The following summer, on July 21, 1900, she gave an interview to the *Oregonian* about a prescient comment that Virgil had made to her about Warren:

While I was visiting my father last winter [in Kirkland, Arizona,] he told me that he had a letter from Warren that he intended to return to Arizona from San Francisco. My father said then, "If Warren ever dies he will be shot. He is too hasty, quick-tempered, and too ready to pick a quarrel. Besides, he will not let bygones be bygones, and on that account I expect that he will meet a violent death."

Indeed, in early July of 1900 Virgil's unfortunate prediction came true. Warren's sister-in-law Allie told her biographer, "Warren—it was too bad about Warren. He went back to Arizona and worked for the Arizona Cattleman's Association and drove a stage between Willcox and Globe. He always had a bad temper when he was drinking, but these weren't often. Just periodicals you might say between trips. In the saloons he'd play cards till he was drunk and then walk up to his enemy, a cowboy named Johnny Boyett, and say, 'Johnny, get out your gun and let's shoot it out.' Then Johnny being afraid would say, 'I haven't got a gun.' And Warren would go back to playin' cards and leave him alone. One day the same thing happened. Warren got drunk and said, 'Johnny, get your gun. We're goin' to shoot it out fair and square!' He forgot, bein' a little tipsy, that this time he had left his gun in the hotel room. Johnny Boyett got his gun, knowin' it, and walked up to Warren. Warren stood up, reached for his gun and found he didn't have any. Then he raised his bare hands and walked right up to the cowboy and Johnny Boyett shot him and killed him. And Boyett was acquitted." Warren died alone in Willcox after Boyett shot him July 6, 1900.

Afterword

The Victorian era, which is when the bulk of the Mrs. Earps were raised and lived, was a challenge all on its own to frontier women. Being Victorian didn't mean one was rich, but rather that one lived by certain social codes. Victorian women, whether rich or poor, were skilled in a variety of etiquettes from fashion and dining to calling and social gatherings, generally following in their mothers' footsteps. It's clear some of the Mrs. Earps' mothers were stern religious ladies and yet others were fallen women.

The harsh reality of living on the frontier often required pioneer women to adapt their lifestyle, depending upon where they lived. It was much easier for a woman and her family to follow a proper Victorian lifestyle if they moved to an existing town or city like Denver or San Francisco. However, take that same family and put them in a rural town or on a ranch somewhere and they had to adjust their living standards.

Rural living didn't automatically equate with a lack of manners and spitting on the floor—although there were some exceptions—but it meant doing without a variety of clothes, fine china, or fancy furniture. One might say women in these circumstances had to "let their hair down"—not because they were scandalous, but because they were practical. Imagine Allie Earp chopping wood in a fancy dress!

The women especially who braved the West not only had to deal with their new surroundings, but also needed to make their eastern US social standards fit in as well. While most western women tried to live up to Victorian standards, sometimes it was downright difficult. On the other hand, some just didn't care.

Even in the eastern US, social standards varied. It is true that a woman living in or near a big eastern city would have handled herself differently than someone residing in the countryside or out west. Granted, the wealthier one was, the more elegant the parties and clothes were. However, lack of money was not an excuse for a lack of social skills.

In western towns where supplies were available, women bought material to make their own clothes, like Allie and Mattie did. In the 1870s, it was a real treat to have a calico dress. Clothing standards, especially for women, were much more relaxed in the rural areas—not necessarily because women wanted to or felt they could be less formal, but because supplies and practicality forced them to. While most eastern women had several dresses for various occasions, many women in the West were lucky to have two. One dress was for daily chores and the other for special occasions, such as church.

In America, no one subject was more important to the Victorians than a general knowledge of manners, rules, ceremonies, and all-around proper etiquette. Those who failed to follow the rules were considered "social monsters." The people in the eastern part of the United States likely considered most of the pioneers living out west social monsters unless they lived in a big city like Denver or San Francisco.

Victorian weddings, unless the family was rich, were generally small ceremonies presided over by a justice of the peace. Some couples did get married at their parents' homes and in churches, but the weddings were nothing like we have today. There were no albums, no books for guests to sign, and no formal wedding gowns. The bride normally wore her best Sunday dress and the groom his best Sunday suit. A honeymoon, if they had one at all, was brief and usually spent near where the couple lived. Finding a record of marriage to prove a wedding took place is extremely difficult. More often than not, the only record remaining of a nineteenth-century marriage is a note in a family Bible.

Verifying the marriages of the Earps proved especially difficult for several reasons. In addition to a lack of official records, the Earps' nomad-like movements, some individuals' lack of memory or the desire to hide certain facts, and fires in county offices or other places where records were kept make it nearly impossible to find even some of the most basic pieces of information. Only two of the Mr. and Mrs. Earps in this book had children, making documents such as letters, mementos, and photos passed down through the generations almost nonexistent. There could be records and documents that have ended up in the hands of cousins or nieces and nephews, such as Louisa's great-nephew, that have yet to be discovered. There could also be some dust-covered gems sitting in the dark storeroom of a remote historical society, waiting to be found. Stories are told and passed down through generations—we all have them. After so many years, it's almost impossible to know which are fact and which are fiction.

Death records often yield valuable clues about a person's history, but alas, these too are difficult to find. When most people in the nineteenth century died they were examined by a coroner and laid to rest, sometimes with a headstone or other type of grave marker. Death certificates weren't usually issued—especially if the deceased had lived in a rural location. Even if a grave marker was placed, it may have been made of wood that rotted, burned, or otherwise was lost. Cemetery records vary and while some do contain details, many do not, other than a name and date of death and interment. Funerals, if they were held, were a private family affair that wouldn't gain a mention—least likely, an obituary—in local newspapers. Such mentions generally were reserved for the well-to-do, famous, or notorious.

In stark contrast to the days of the Wild West, today's online world preserves and makes accessible even the most obscure trivia. People take pictures by the hundreds or even thousands and post them online, write blogs about their daily lives, and tweet or post to

Facebook constantly. One hundred years from now, it's quite likely that more stories, photos, and memories will have been preserved than anyone could ever imagine. Such is not the case from one hundred years in the past. Photos were not easily taken and they weren't cheap. Writing implements required inkwells, and the only way to correspond was to write a letter or send a telegram. Very few people needed or had any type of printed identification—all making research a difficult task. As long as our cyber world exists, we will all be easily remembered for centuries to come. Nevertheless, it's doubtless that verifying the accuracy of any information will continue to challenge researchers. And so the task of the historian continues. . . .

ENDNOTES

1 – *Los Angeles Herald,* February 3, 1887.
2 – Brown, Clara S., *Tombstone Letters of Clara Brown,* Riverside, California: Earl Chafin Press, 1988, pages 41-45.
3 – *Southwest Missourian,* February 24, 1870, p. 3.
4 – Lamar County records, Book A, p. 732.
5 – Research from Gary L. Roberts.
6 – Tefertiller, *Wyatt Earp: The Life Behind the Legend,* New York: John Wiley & Sons, 1997.
7 – Jerry Blaylock, Rootsweb,archiver.rootsweb.ancestry.com/th/read/ BLALOCK/2001-02/0981972091, last accessed February 10, 2013.
8 – Ann Kirschner, *Lady at the OK Corral,* New York: HarperCollins, 2013.
9 – Details taken from the 1900 US census.
10 – *San Francisco Bulletin,* June 19, 1869.
11 – Henry G. Langley, *San Francisco Directory,* October 1868.
12 – Mabel Earp Cason and Vinnolia Earp Ackerman, *The Cason Manuscript,* edited by Earl Chafin (Riverside, CA: Earl Chafin Press). Unpublished. Cited with specific permission of the Cason family.
13 – Carol Mitchell, "The Lady Sadie," True West, February/March 2001.
14 – Ibid.
15 – *San Francisco Bulletin,* June 24, 1880.
16 – Research by Roger Jay.
17 – *Arizona Weekly Miner,* December 26, 1879.
18 – Mitchell, "The Lady Sadie."
19 – Ibid.
20 – *Arizona Weekly Miner,* May 15, 1874.
21 – US census, August 6, 1870, California, Sacramento, 2nd Ward Sacramento, Series M593, Roll 77, p. 233. Burton, Julia, 49, Keeping house. United States Census, June 3, 1880, Arizona, Yavapai, Prescott, Series T9, Roll 37, Page 448. Burton, Julia, 60, Housekeeper.
22 – *The Cason Manuscript.*
23 – *Arizona Weekly Miner,* April 9 and 16, 1875.
24 – Mitchell, "The Lady Sadie."
25 – *The Cason Manuscript,* p. 87.
26 – District Court of Yavapai County, Victoria F. Behan v. John H. Behan, Docket #275, May 22, 1875.
27 – Research courtesy of Roger Jay.
28 – Mitchell, "The Lady Sadie."

29 – *The Cason Manuscript,* p. 87.
30 – Original letter at the Arizona Historical Society, Tucson. Quote cited in Kirschner, Lady at the OK Corral.
31 – *Galveston Daily News,* December 1 and 23, 1883.
32 – Tefertiller, *Wyatt Earp.*
33 – Kirschner, *Lady at the OK Corral.*
34 – Tefertiller, *Wyatt Earp.*
35 – findagrave.com/cgi-bin/fg.cgi?page=gr&GRid=40289019.
36 – *Omaha Daily Bee,* December 31, 1872.
37 – *Arizona Daily Star,* May 30, 1882.
38 – 1880 US census.
39 – Agnes Houston Cebell, Louisa's younger sister.
40 – Nicholas P. and Virginia A. Earp, parents of Morgan Earp.
41 – Bashford Waughtal, Louisa's cousin. Bashford was the son of Samuel Baughman Waughtal.
42 – Louisa's older sister Olive Knudsen.
43 – Elizabeth Houston Hanley, Louisa's youngest sister. The family called her Bessie.
44 – Elizabeth Waughtal Houston, Louisa's mother.
45 – Catherine Houston Robinson, Louisa's younger sister.
46 – The Houston family moved from Iowa to Minnesota in 1880.
47 – Louisa's oldest sister, Olive, married Peter Knudsen and went to Minnesota with the Houston family.
48 – Agnes Houston married August Cebell on February 13, 1881.
49 – Mason City, Iowa.
50 – Adelia Earp Edwards, Morgan Earp's sister.
51 – Letter was probably written to her sister Catherine Houston Robinson.
52 – Forrestine Hooker, *An Arizona Vendetta,* edited and transcribed by Earl Chafin, Riverside, CA: Earl Chafin Press, 1998, pp. 33–37.
53 – *Tombstone Epitaph,* March 20, 1882.
54 – Chafin, *Tombstone Letters of Clara Brown,* p. 47.
55 – Adelia Earp-Edwards, *Wild West Remembrances,* edited by Earl Chafin (Riverside, CA: Earl Chafin Press, 2000). Courtesy of Kenneth Vail.
56 – Louisa was married to Gustav H. Peters in California on December 31, 1885.
57 – Louisa's mother's brothers, Daniel B. Waughtal and Frederick Waughtal.
58 – Anne Collier, "Harriett 'Hattie' Catchim," *WOLA Journal,* Summer 2007.
59 – *Cleveland* (Ohio) *Leader* via the *San Francisco Chronicle.*
60 – Herbert Asbury, *The Barbary Coast,* New York: Alfred A. Knopf, 1933.
61 – *San Diego Union,* August 15, 1893.
62 – *Arizona Sentinel,* November 25, 1893.

BIBLIOGRAPHY

Chafin, Earl, ed. *Tombstone Letters of Clara Brown*. Riverside, CA: Earl Chafin Press, 1988.

Collier, Anne. "Harriett 'Hattie' Catchim: A Controversial Earp Family Member," *WOLA Journal*, Summer 2007.

Earp-Edwards, Adelia; edited by Earl Chafin. *Wild West Remembrances*. Riverside, CA: Earl Chafin Press, 2000

Gatto, Steve. www.wyattearp.net, last accessed January 20, 2013.

Hooker, Forrestine C.; edited and transcribed by Earl Chafin. *An Arizona Vendetta: The Truth About Wyatt Earp*. Riverside, CA: Earl Chafin Press, 1998.

Jay, Roger. "Face to Face: Sadie Mansfield/Josephine Sarah Marcus." *Wild West History Journal*, February 2013.

Miller, Nyle H., and Joseph W. Snell. *Why the West Was Wild*. Oklahoma City: University of Oklahoma Press, 2003.

Mitchell, Carole. "Lady Sadie," *True West* magazine, February/March 2001.

Tefertiller, Casey. *Wyatt Earp: The Life Behind the Legend*. New York: John Wiley & Son, 1997.

Waters, Frank. *Tombstone Travesty*. Unpublished manuscript.

"Wyatt Earp's Lost Years," *Wild West* magazine, June 2012.

Index

About the Author

Sherry Monahan is the author of several books on the Victorian West, including *California Vines; Wines & Pioneers; Taste of Tombstone; Pikes Peak; The Wicked West: Boozers, Cruisers, Gamblers, and More;* and *Tombstone's Treasure: Silver Mines & Golden Saloons.*

In addition to her writing, Sherry is the "Genie with a Bottle." In this role, she traces the genealogy of food and wine. She calls it Winestry and says, "History never tasted so good."

She recently finished writing *Her Fateful Decisions,* which is the remarkable true story of an upper-class family who settled the rugged land of Lake County, California, in the 1880s. Their motive was to gain back the money they lost in England, but these high-society aristocrats preferred cricket, boating, and acting over the chores of farming.

Sherry has appeared on the History Channel in many shows, including *Cowboys and Outlaws: Wyatt Earp, Lost Worlds: Sin City of the West (Deadwood), Investigating History,* and two of the *Wild West Tech* shows. She received a Wrangler in the Western Heritage Awards for her performance in the show *Cowboys and Outlaws* in 2010.

She has her own column called Frontier Fare and is a contributing editor for *True West* magazine. Other publications include the *Tombstone Times, Tombstone Tumbleweed, Tombstone Epitaph, Arizona*

Highways, and other freelance works. She was a contributor to *The Best of the Best of Arizona* and *Encyclopedia of Prostitution and Sex Work.*

Sherry is the incoming president of Western Writers of America and holds memberships in the following organizations: Women Writing the West, the Authors Guild, Wild West History Association, Association of Professional Genealogists, and Westerners International. She is also a charter member of the National Women's History Museum.

In addition to her writing, Sherry works as marketing consultant and professional genealogist.